BERKLEE BEGINNING GUITAR

Kim Perlak

Berklee Press

I0806974

BERKLEE PRESS

Editor in Chief: Jonathan Feist

Senior Vice President Pre-College, Online, and Professional Programs/
CEO and Cofounder of Berklee Online: Debbie Cavalier

ISBN 978-0-87639-228-7

Berklee
Press

1140 Boylston Street
Boston, MA 02215-3693 USA
(617) 747-2146

Visit Berklee Press Online at
www.berkleepress.com

Berklee Online

Study music online at
online.berklee.edu

Distributed By

HAL•LEONARD®
A Muse Group Company

Visit Hal Leonard Online
www.halleonard.com

Berklee Press, a publishing activity of Berklee College of Music, is a not-for-profit educational publisher.
Available proceeds from the sales of our products are contributed to the scholarship funds of the college.

CONTENTS

ACKNOWLEDGMENTS

My students made this book possible. Years ago, when I first began teaching, my students showed me what made sense as they picked up the instrument—and what didn't. Hours, days, weeks, months, and years of working with players across the country, and around the world, taught me to be a teacher. Thank you, in particular, to my students from the National Guitar Workshop; my time in Austin, TX; and at Berklee Online in the *Guitar Fundamentals* course. We lived together on the guitar and honed the approach of this book. Thank you to my friend and colleague, Berklee professor Amanda Monaco, who has been a teaching partner in this material, years ago and today.

Thank you to my colleagues in the Berklee College of Music Guitar Department, which I am proud to lead with Assistant Chair Sheryl Bailey, Chair Emeritus Larry Baione, Associate Dean Karen Bell, Interim Dean Sean Skeete, and BCM Executive Director and Vice President Ron Savage. Their openness and respect for all styles, and for students of all backgrounds and levels, inspires my work on the guitar and our work together. Thank you, as always, to our editor-in-chief, Jonathan Feist, for his practical insight, and to our colleagues at Berklee Online for welcoming more and more players to our Berklee guitar community.

ABOUT THIS BOOK

I love the guitar. In my thirty years of teaching, one of my greatest joys has been to guide others who are inspired to play. In classrooms, workshops, and lessons around the world, my students have taught me as we've explored the technique, theory, and expressive aspects of guitar music. The curriculum in this book is a result of our ongoing work together.

This book lays a comprehensive foundation of playing, guitar knowledge, and musicianship that will get you playing right away, and that you can take into different styles. Within a group of "beginners," there will be players of varying age and experience—from those who have just picked up the instrument, to those who come from a self-taught or lesson background and are looking to fill in gaps. Think of this book as your guide through years of guitar practice at your personal level. At times, your conceptual understanding of the material may be ahead of your technical comfort level—and at other times, the opposite may be true for you. This book will help you understand what you are playing as well as how to play it.

Part I covers the basics of technique, music theory, reading, and improvisation that will allow you to play popular and traditional music, and set the building blocks for jazz and classical styles. Part II explores the music theory, applications, and techniques that will expand your playing options. Part III moves beyond these basics, and invites you to open more creative doors. Part IV includes practice materials similar to many songs you may recognize, making them useful to learn!

Learning the guitar is a cumulative, lifelong endeavor. Revisit the basics each day that you practice. Take your time as you progress: solidify topics that are familiar, and move slowly with materials that are unfamiliar. The stronger your foundation, the more fluid your playing—both technically and expressively. In the Berklee Guitar Department, we believe that a strong foundation on our instrument will lead you to creative freedom in the styles you love.

Enjoy the process, take some creative chances, and remember to breathe!

Welcome to the guitar, and to Berklee.

—Kim Perlak, 2024

Part I

Guitar Basics

The chapters in part I will guide you through the basics of playing popular and traditional songs as both a rhythm and lead guitarist. Chapter 1 covers your setup: guitar parts, posture, technique, and breathing. Chapter 2 presents the foundations of rhythm guitar playing: bass lines, chart reading, the moveable "power" chord, and strumming patterns. Chapter 3 introduces lead guitar playing with a moveable scale pattern and exercises for expression. Chapter 4 is an overview of standard and tablature notation. As you approach these materials, take each one slowly in regular, consistent practice.

CHAPTER 1

Setup Basics

PARTS OF THE GUITAR

All types of guitars—electric, acoustic, classical—share the same basic parts. They are: head, nut, neck, frets, body, and bridge. Different types of acoustic guitars have sound holes and soundboards, and electric guitars have volume and tone knobs, pickups, often a pickup switch, a cable jack, and sometimes a whammy bar.

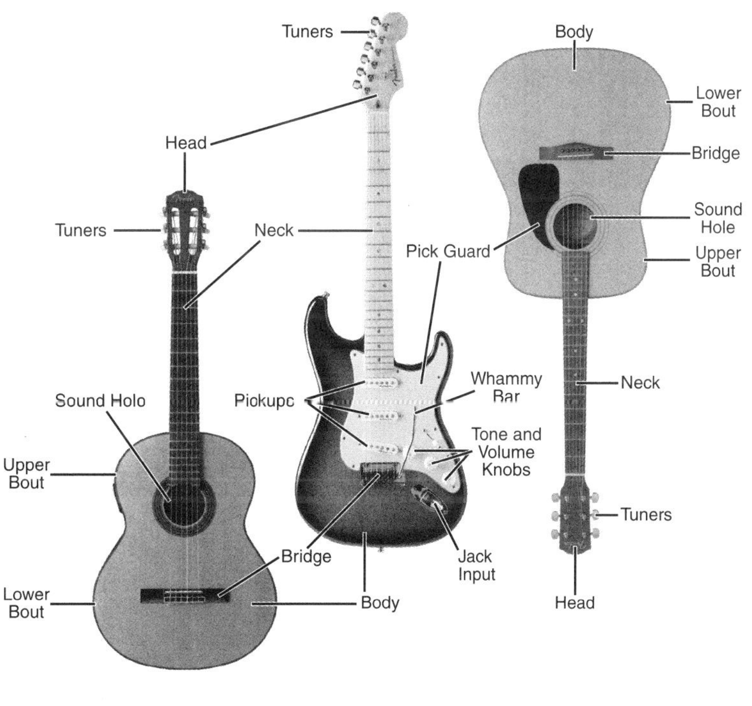

FIG. 1.1. Parts of the Guitar

The type of strings on each kind of guitar (nylon, electric steel, acoustic steel) affect the tone of the instrument, the technique you'll use to play it, and the way you'll change the strings. In the beginning stages, look to a more experienced player for assistance in string-changing.

TOOLS: TUNER AND METRONOME

Invest in two tools for daily practice: an electronic tuner and a metronome. Both can be found as devices or as apps on a smart phone. The tuner will guide your ear in keeping your strings tuned. The metronome will help you play steadily—as a soloist and with others.

"RIGHT-HANDED" VS. "LEFT-HANDED" GUITARS

The majority of guitars are made "right-handed," meaning that your right hand will pluck the strings (with fingers or a pick), and your left hand will fret the notes on the neck. While most left-handed players use a "right-handed" instrument, some choose a "left-handed" guitar, which is inverted so that the right hand frets the notes and the left hand picks. In this book, we'll refer to "fretting hand" and "picking hand" to accommodate both approaches.

"UP" AND "DOWN"

Moving "up" or "down" the guitar neck follows the direction of the pitch, not the direction of gravity. The frets on the neck are counted from the nut, beginning with the number 1. "Moving *up* the neck" means that you will move your fretting hand from the nut towards the body of the guitar. The strings are numbered ⑥ to ①, with the thickest and lowest sounding string numbered as ⑥. The "low" strings ⑥ to ④ will be those closest to the ceiling.

The only time in which "down is down" in guitar playing is when you are strumming. A "down" strum means that your picking hand moves across the strings on a diagonal towards the floor. On an "up strum," your picking hand moves across the strings on a diagonal towards the ceiling. Figure 1.2 and the horizontal fretboard diagrams in this book show your perspective when holding the guitar, tilting it towards yourself to see the fretboard. A "down strum" moves across the strings from "low" to "high," string ⑥ to ①—from the bottom towards the top of the diagrams.

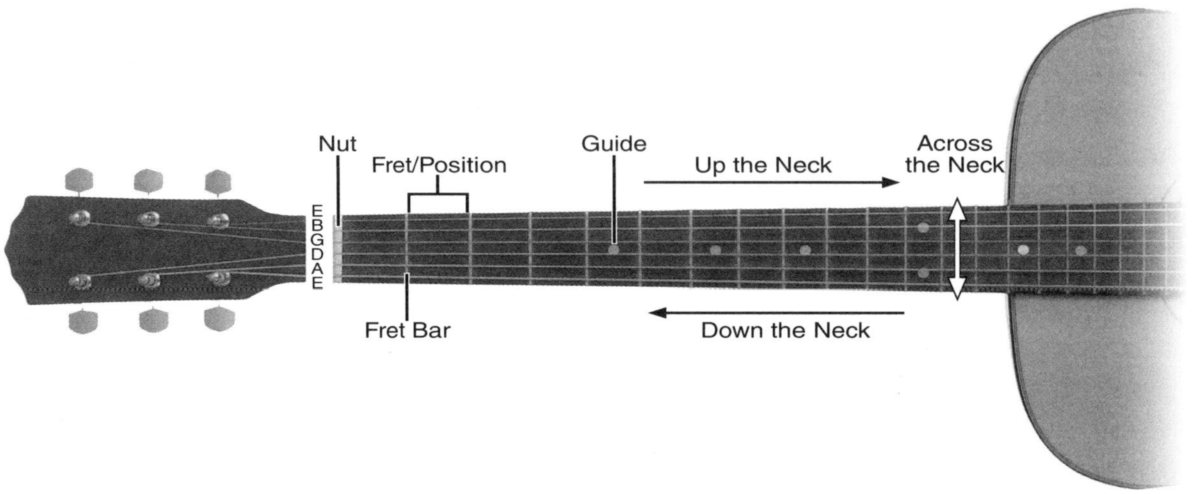

FIG. 1.2. Neck Navigation

POSITION

Most electric and acoustic guitar players sit with the guitar resting on their "picking-hand leg." Classical guitar players generally sit with the guitar on the "fretting-hand" leg to facilitate movement on the guitar neck. Raise the leg that you put the guitar on by using a footstool, or if your guitar is on the picking-hand leg, cross that leg over your other. Bring the upper bout of the guitar's body central to your chest. If you prefer to stand and use a guitar strap, adjust the strap to bring the instrument into position.

Acoustic

Electric

Classical

Standing

FIG. 1.3. Holding the Guitar

Fretting-Hand Position

The fingers on the fretting hand are numbered: index = 1 (first), middle = 2 (second), ring = 3 (third), pinky = 4 (fourth).

Position the four fingers of your fretting hand on the neck on one string so that each finger "gets a fret." The second and third fingers will be positioned "straight on," while the first finger will naturally lean toward the head of the guitar, and the fourth finger will lean toward the body. Your fretting-hand wrist should be slightly curved outwards to align the hand. Your thumb's main job is balance and should generally rest on the back of the guitar neck between fingers 1 and 2.

Curved Fingers

Top View of Fingertips

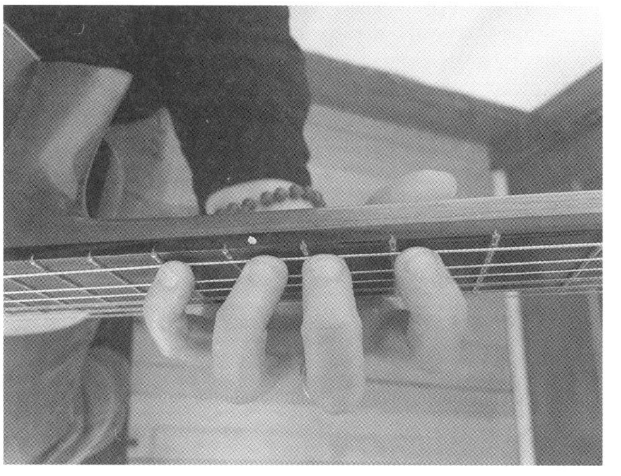

FIG. 1.4. Fretting Hand

Picking-Hand Position

The fingers of the picking hand are labeled with lowercase letters: thumb = *p*, index = *i*, middle = *m*, ring = *a*, and pinky = *c*. (The pinky finger is seldom indicated in picking.)

Find your basic picking-hand position by draping your right arm across the body of the guitar on a diagonal. There are three wrist motions that make a difference in the general picking-hand position: angle, height, and tilt. With angle, aim for a straight wrist, aligning your hand with your arm. For height, make sure the big knuckles of your hand are higher or at the same height as your wrist joint. With tilt, rotate your hand and forearm as if you are turning a doorknob. Tilt your hand toward the pinky-side to support your weaker fingers. Together, these elements of alignment result in healthy technique and a full sound.

Acoustic, Pick

Acoustic, Fingerstyle (Front)

Acoustic, Fingerstyle (Top)

Electric, Pick (Front)

Electric, Pick (Top)

FIG. 1.5. Picking-Hand Position, from Different Angles

Holding the Pick

In this chapter, we'll play with a pick, and we'll cover fingerstyle techniques in chapter 8. To hold the pick, curve the fingers of your picking hand towards your palm and place the pick on the tip joint of your index finger. Make sure the pointed part of the pick is facing out. Secure the pick with the tip joint of your thumb.

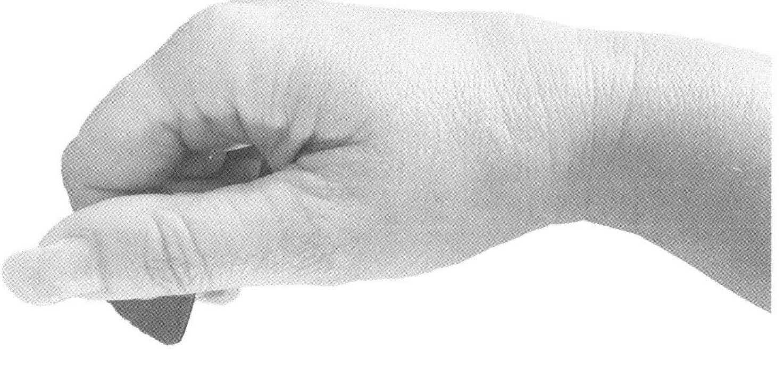

FIG. 1.6. Holding the Pick

BREATHING

Breathing is an essential part of guitar technique. As you set up with the guitar each day, take a deep breath. As you exhale, pay attention to how your shoulders, arms, and hands feel. Breathe consciously as you practice, and allow yourself to become more and more aware of when you hold your breath: when you are concentrating? when you are nervous? when you are judging your progress? Breathing allows us to relax on the instrument, allowing for fluid playing, creative awareness, and injury prevention.

PRACTICE: WARM-UP EXERCISES

Every day when you pick up the guitar, warm up slowly with physical exercises to become more comfortable with your technique. Set your metronome at a slow click—no higher than 60 beats per minute. Lock in your strumming and note playing, one strum or note per click. Play with fluid and relaxed motions, listen to your tone, and remember to breathe.

Alternate-Picking Practice for Strumming

1. Sit or stand with your guitar in a comfortable, aligned posture.
2. Hold the pick between your thumb and *i* finger of your picking hand.
3. Strum all of the strings down (towards the floor) and up (towards the ceiling) in one large motion, allowing all of the strings to sound. Strum on a diagonal line, away from your body as you strum down towards the floor. This will prevent your pick from getting stuck in between the strings.

Before Strum

After Strum

FIG. 1.7. Strumming Position

On the down-strums, play strongly, sounding all the strings, and play lighter on the up-strums.

Notice how tightly you need to hold the pick while you are strumming.

Alternate-Picking Practice for Single Notes

1. Hold the pick between your thumb and *i* finger of your picking hand.
2. On the first string, ①, slowly play the string down (towards the floor) and up (towards the ceiling), in even, relaxed motions. Alternating between down and up strokes like this is called "alternate picking." Make each note sound even in length and volume.
3. Then play on the second string, ②, and so on.

"Fretting-Hand Walking"

1. Go to the 5th fret on the guitar, and put your first finger on string ⑥.
2. Position your finger comfortably, pressing in the fret just behind the fret bar, and checking your overall fretting-hand position. Play that note with your pick.
3. Then hop your first finger to string ⑤ in the same fret, set it up comfortably, and play that note.
4. Continue with each string from ⑥ to ①, and then move back across the strings in that fret from ① to ⑥.
5. Next, lift your first finger off the string. Position your second finger in the 6th fret, and repeat the exercise.
6. Continue with your third finger in the 7th fret, and your fourth in the 8th fret.

CHAPTER 2

Rhythm Guitar Basics

In popular guitar styles, rhythm guitar parts create texture and groove. At a basic level, these parts are made up of bass lines, chord shapes, and strumming patterns. This chapter presents rhythm guitar foundation that will allow you to play with others right away—while grounding you in basic techniques, music theory, and fretboard knowledge. To start, you'll need to understand the relationship between two pieces of information: the musical alphabet and the names of the strings on the guitar.

MUSICAL ALPHABET

The musical alphabet is made up of seven letters: A, B, C, D, E, F, G. These notes are considered the "natural" notes because they are identified by their letter name alone. The distance between each consecutive natural notes of the musical alphabet is known as a "step." There are two types of steps: *half steps* and *whole steps*. In the musical alphabet, there are two half steps, one between the notes E and F, and another between B and C. All other consecutive notes in the musical alphabet are separated by a whole step.

On a single guitar string, the distance of a half step is one fret—for example: fret 1 to fret 2. The distance of a whole step is two frets—for example: fret 1 to fret 3.

The note names of the six guitar strings when they are played *open*, without fretting a note, are: ⑥ = E, ⑤ = A, ④ = D, ③ = G, ② = B, ① = E.

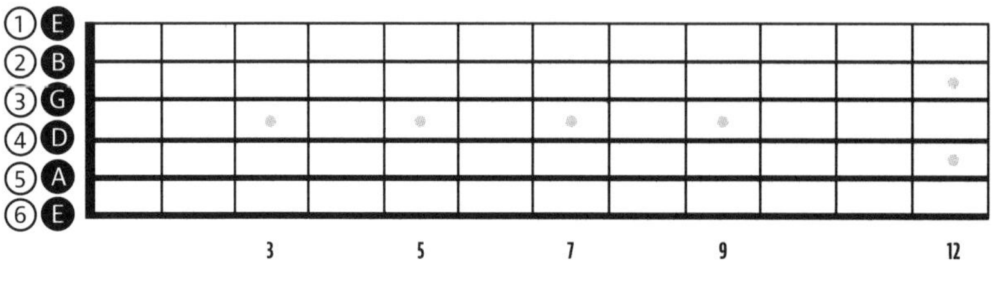

FIG. 2.1. Notes of the Open Strings

NATURAL NOTES ON STRING ⑥

Apply these two pieces of information to string ⑥, and you can name the natural notes on each fret of that string. Begin on the open note E, and ascend the neck with your first finger on your fretting hand by half or whole step, as appropriate.

The natural notes and their frets on string ⑥ are:

⑥	Fret:	0	1	2	3	4	5	6	7	8	9	10	11	12
	Note:	E	F		G		A		B	C		D		E

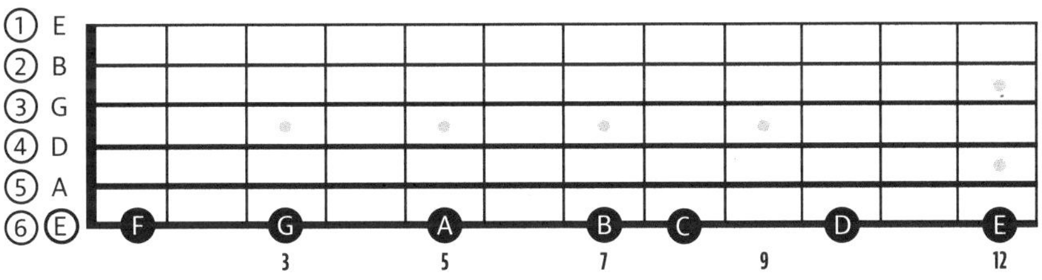

FIG. 2.2. Natural Notes on ⑥

SHARPS AND FLATS

Sharps and flats indicate notes that fall on the frets that are "in between" each note of a whole step in the musical alphabet, as "altered" versions of that note. A note that is a half-step above a note in the musical alphabet is called a "sharp," and is indicated with this symbol: ♯. A note that is a half-step below a note in the musical alphabet is called a "flat" and is indicated with a flat sign: ♭. Because of this, you'll notice that the notes on these "in between" frets have two names. A note will be called F♯ or G♭, for example, depending on the context.

The frets and note names of the sharps and flats on string ⑥ are:

⑥	Fret:	0	1	2	3	4	5	6	7	8	9	10	11	12
	Note:	E	F	F♯ or G♭	G	G♯ or A♭	A	A♯ or B♭	B	C	C♯ or D♭	D	D♯ or E♭	E

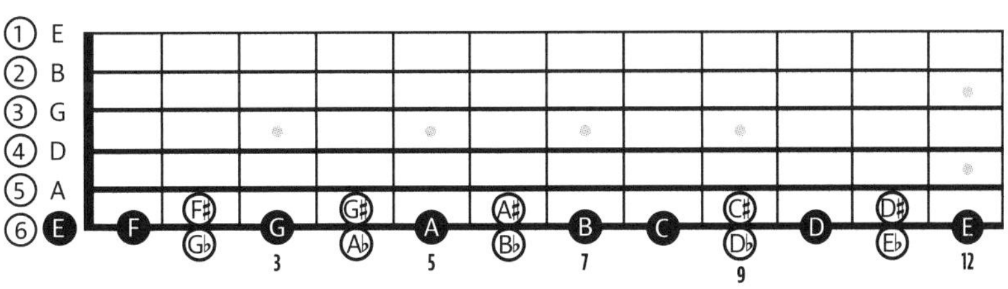

FIG. 2.3. All Notes on ⑥

PRACTICE: PLAYING THE NOTES ON STRING ⑥

Play the notes in the following examples in succession on string ⑥, fretting them with your first finger. As you play, be aware of your hand position and your sound. As you shift your fretting hand up and down the neck, use a relaxed motion, and look ahead to the next fret before you shift. Move your hand to your eyes! Once you are familiar with these note locations, create your own melodies with notes on string ⑥.

1. C G F A C
2. G D A C
3. E♭ G A♭ B♭
4. A C♯ D A

RHYTHM BASICS: PLAYING CHARTS "IN 4"

Now that you are familiar with the notes on string ⑥, you're ready to read charts. A "chart" is a type of written music that shows you what to play and when to play it. We'll start with the most basic type of chart, called a "chord chart," and use figures 2.4 and 2.5 as examples.

The chart in figure 2.4, "Heaven," is divided into four units, called "measures" or "bars." The symbol on the left is called a "time signature." When musicians are "playing in time," they are establishing a constant rhythmic count repeated through the chart. The top number of the time signature indicates how many beats or counts are in each bar. This chart is counted "in 4," meaning that you will count four beats per bar as you play: "1, 2, 3, 4." When you lock your playing into the rhythmic repetition of this count, you are playing "in time" and "in 4." The majority of popular and traditional charts are played "in 4."

The letters within each bar refer to chords and are called "chord symbols." When there is only one chord symbol in the bar, it lasts for the full duration. If there are two chord symbols in a bar, divide the bar in half, unless it is otherwise indicated. Take a look at chart 2.5, "Watchtower." The slash marks underneath the chord symbols in each bar indicate the duration of each. In the second bar, the first chord lasts for three beats and the second chord lasts for one beat. Double lines with dots at the beginning and end of the line are "repeat signs," which indicate that you repeat the material between these signs.

Guitarists read chord charts by playing a form of the chord or the bass note—the "root" of the chords—"in time" (to a constant count of 4). This is the way that multiple players in a band play different rhythm guitar parts using the same basic chord charts. When you play the bass note alone, you are creating a basic bass line.

To play "Heaven" with a basic bass line, you'll use the notes you practiced on string ⑥. First, find each of these bass notes: G, D, A, C on string ⑥, and practice shifting to each note. Then set your metronome to 60 bpm. Listen to a full count of four beats (clicks), and then play the chart. In the first bar, you'll play G on the first beat and D on the third beat. In the second measure, you'll play A on the first beat and hold it for four beats.

Heaven

4/4 ||: G D | Amin | G D | C :||

1 (2) 3 (4) 1 (2) (3) (4)

FIG. 2.4. Chart in 4, "Heaven"

To play "Watchtower," use the slashes as your guide to divide the chords in the second bar unequally, playing them on beats 1 and 4.

Watchtower

4/4 ||: Amin G | F G :||

/ / / / / / / /

1 (2) 3 (4) 1 (2) (3) 4

FIG. 2.5. Chart with Unequal Values, "Watchtower"

"STRONG BEAT" AND "BACKBEAT"

When you are playing "in time" and "in 4," you can create different "pulses," "grooves," or "time feels" based on which beats you emphasize. A "strong beat" pulse emphasizes beats 1 and 3, and is common to the styles of folk/rock, metal, and classical. A "backbeat" groove emphasizes beats 2 and 4, and is common to the styles of blues, R&B, soul, jazz, and classic rock.

In figure 2.6, the beats to emphasize for each time feel are indicated with accent marks in the count below the chart. Practice these by setting your metronome to 60 bpm or lower, with a click on each beat. Play your bass line notes, one on each beat, and play the accented notes louder to create each time feel.

Heaven

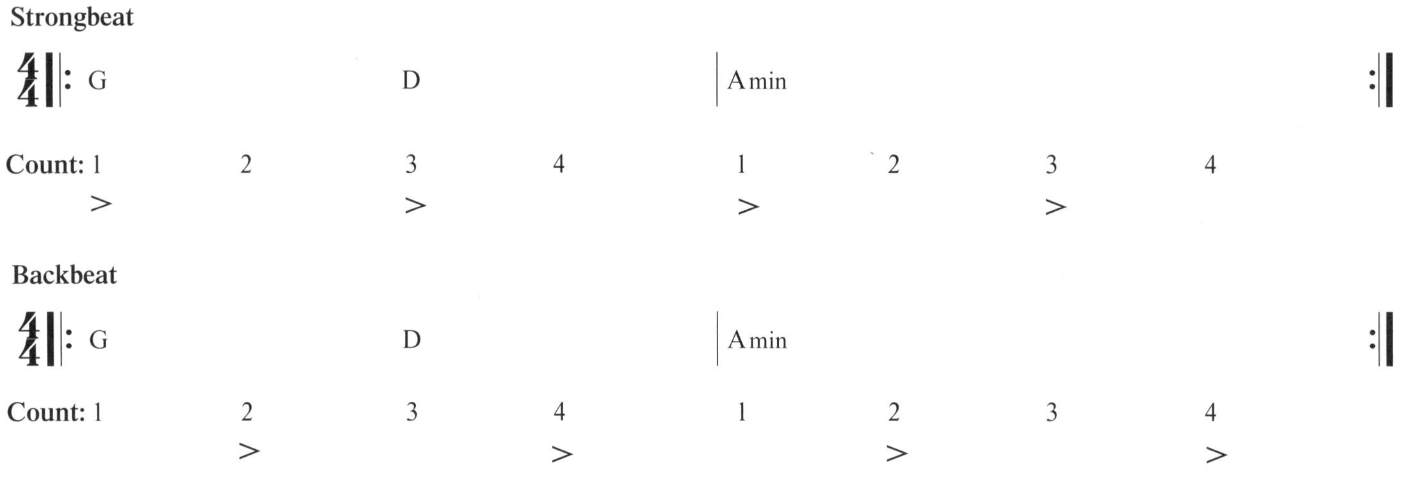

FIG. 2.6. Strongbeat/Backbeat Pulse and Groove, "Heaven"

POWER CHORDS: ROOTS ON STRING ⑥

A "power chord" is a common chord type played on the low strings. Power chords have a dark, powerful sound. In their most standard form, these chords are played with a moveable two-finger shape, rooted on the bass notes you have learned on string ⑥. To build a power chord, fret the root note of the chord on string ⑥ with your first finger. Fret the note on string ⑤ two frets above the root with finger 3 or 4. When you strum the chord, play only the strings you're holding down.

In charts, power chords are indicated with a capital letter and the number "5," for example: G5, A5, C5. The capital letter refers to the root note you will play on string ⑥. The 5 means that the other note of the chord is five notes higher than the root in the scale—more on that theory in chapter 7! Notice that figure 2.7 shows a vertical view of the fretboard, with the lower strings towards the left. This is a common way to illustrate chords.

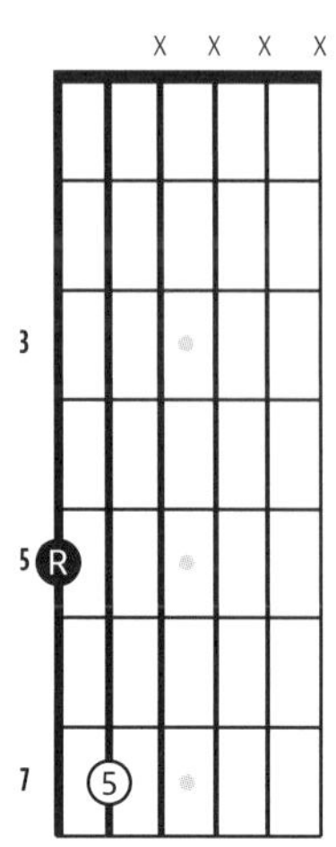

FIG. 2.7. A5, Root on ⑥

In a chart, the songwriter or arranger can specify a power chord by writing the power chord symbols, like: A5, C5. If you are reading a chart with chord symbols written as capital letters and capital letters with lowercase letters or numbers—such as A, Amin, or A7—you can substitute power chords to create a dark, bass-like sound. Knowing power chords will allow you to play charts with chord symbols you haven't yet learned.

Take a look at the charts for "Heaven" and "Watchtower" in figure 2.8 and 2.9, written in their original chord notation and specifically with power chord symbols. Play through these charts using power chords. First, practice each chord change and shift slowly. Once you are comfortable with the sequence, play "in time." First, strum on each chord change and count the beats. Next, strum once on each beat and emphasize the strong beat, and then the backbeat to work on your time feel.

Heaven

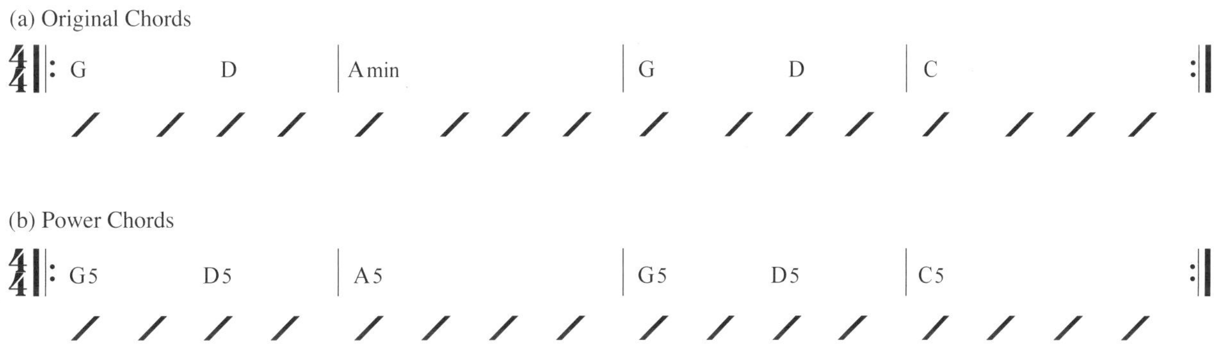

FIG. 2.8. "Heaven" (a) with Original Chord Symbols and (b) with Power Chord Symbols

Watchtower

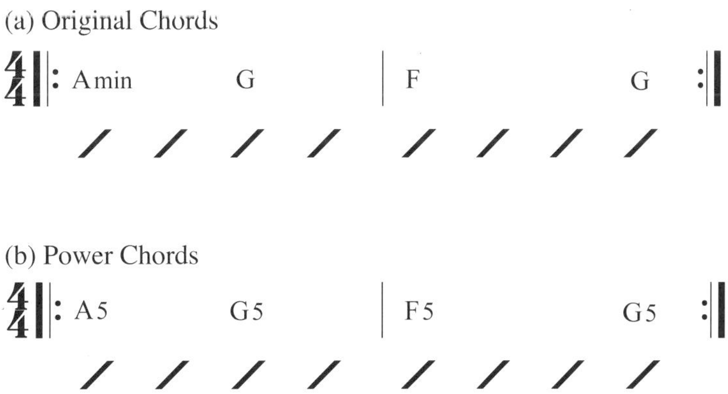

FIG. 2.9. "Watchtower" (a) with Original Chord Symbols and (b) with Power Chord Symbols

NOTES ON STRING ⑤

Now that you're playing bass lines and power chords based on string ⑥, let's look at the same materials based on string ⑤. This will give you more options for note and power chord location, and will allow you to play charts without as much shifting up and down the fretboard.

The natural notes on string ⑤ are:

⑤	Fret:	0	1	2	3	4	5	6	7	8	9	10	11	12
	Note:	A		B	C		D		E	F		G		A

The sharps and flats on string ⑤ are:

⑤	Fret:	0	1	2	3	4	5	6	7	8	9	10	11	12
	Note:	A	A♯ or B♭	B	C	C♯ or D♭	D	D♯ or E♭	E	F	F♯ or G♭	G	G♯ or A♭	A

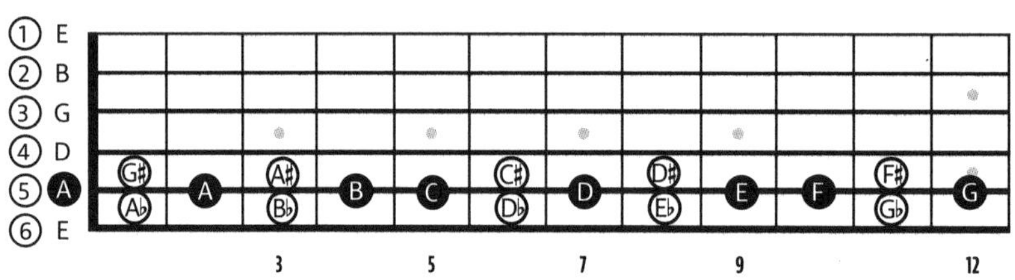

FIG. 2.10. Notes on String ⑤

PRACTICE: PLAYING THE NOTES ON STRING ⑤ AND ON ⑤⑥

Practice the note examples you learned on string ⑥, this time on string ⑤. Play with awareness of your position, shifting, and tone production. Name each note, and memorize its fret-number location. Once you become familiar with the note locations, create your own melodies with the notes on string ⑤.

1. C G F A C
2. G D A C
3. E♭ G A♭ B♭
4. A C♯ D A

Next, use strings ⑤ and ⑥ to play these examples. Move slowly as you shift "across" strings ⑤ and ⑥.

1.	C	G	F	A	C
	⑤	⑥	⑥	⑥	⑤
2.	G	D	A	C	
	⑥	⑤	⑥	⑤	
3.	E♭	G	A♭	B♭	
	⑤	⑥	⑥	⑥	
4.	A	C♯	D	A	
	⑥	⑤	⑤	⑥	

POWER CHORDS: ROOTS ON STRING ⑤

To play a power chord rooted on string ⑤, move your power chord shape over by one string. Fret the "root" of the chord with finger 1 on string ⑤. Fret the second note on string ④, two frets above the root, with finger 3 or 4. Remember: when you strum the chord, play only the strings you're holding down.

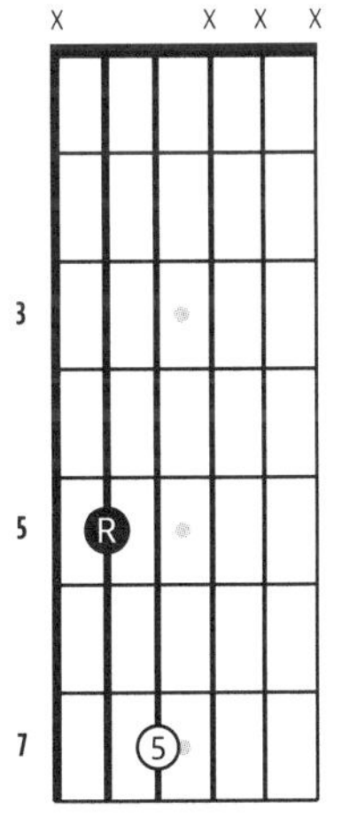

FIG. 2.11. D5 Power Chord with Root on String ⑤

Knowing power chords with the roots on both strings ⑥ and ⑤ will allow you to play charts without as much shifting up and down the neck. Instead, you'll often shift "across" the strings to change chords, while staying in the same position on the fretboard.

PRACTICE: POWER CHORDS ON STRINGS ⑥ AND ⑤

Practice "Heaven" and the new chart, "Wisdom," fretting the power chords on strings ⑥ and ⑤ as indicated. Notice the technical difference of shifting across the strings, instead of moving only up and down the fretboard. Most sheet music doesn't include string numbers; you must make these decisions yourself!

Heaven

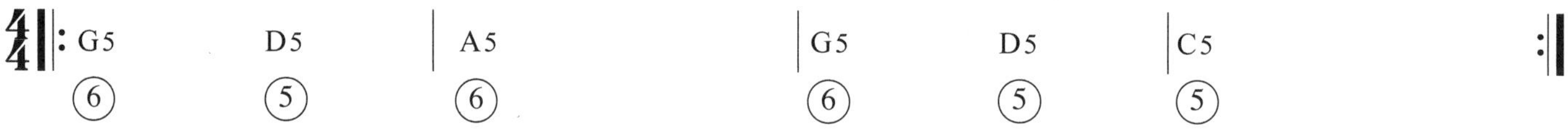

FIG. 2.12. "Heaven" with Power Chord Roots Marked

Wisdom

FIG. 2.13. "Wisdom" with Power Chord Roots Marked

RHYTHMIC NOTATION BASICS

An overview of rhythmic notation basics will help you read and write rhythm guitar parts "in time." This overview of rhythmic notation is just the beginning of your long-term study. For in-depth work with rhythmic notation, please see *Berklee Contemporary Music Theory* by Vessela Stoyanova and Jeff Perry, or *Berklee Music Theory* (Book 1) by Paul Schmeling.

Take a look at this chart of basic rhythmic values and their notation.

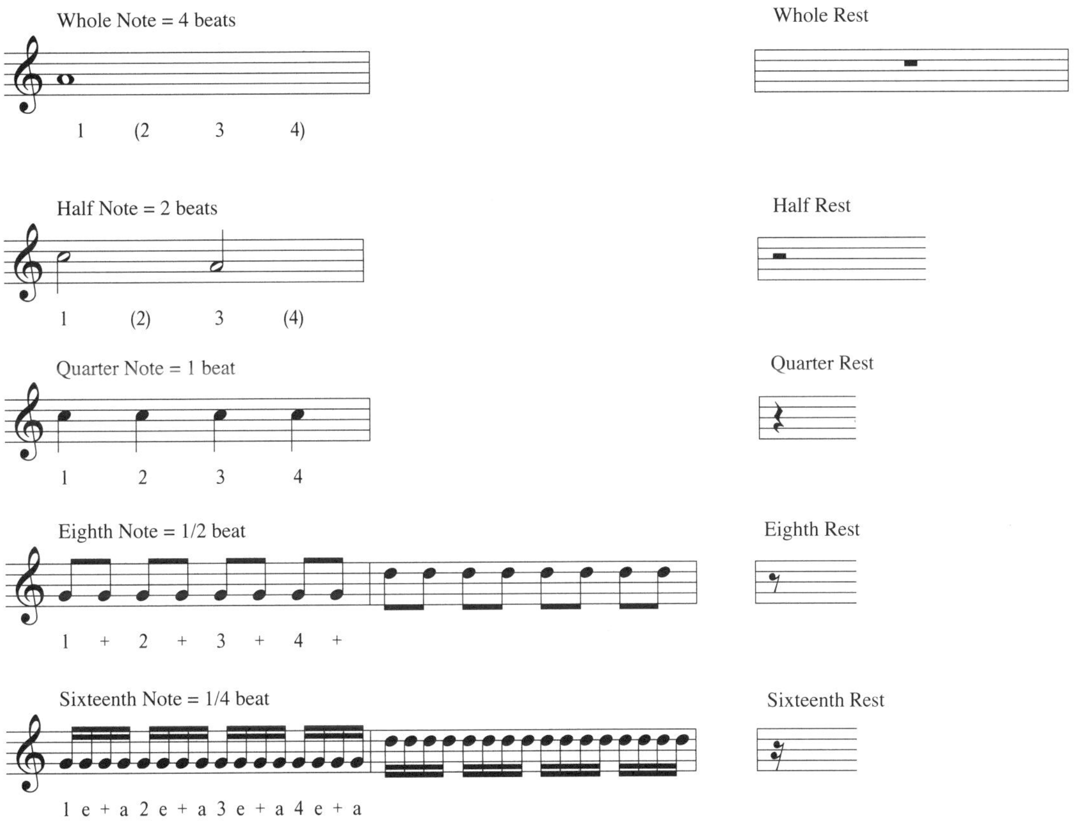

FIG. 2.14. Rhythm and Rest Values Chart

The basic rhythmic durations for "playing in four" are whole, half, quarter, eighth, and sixteenth notes. When playing in "four," the whole note gets four beats, the half note gets two beats, and the quarter note gets one beat.

A dot placed next to any of these notes increases its duration by half of its value. For example, the dotted half note gets three beats.

Earlier in this chapter, when you played the "Heaven" and "Watchtower" charts, you realized each of these rhythmic values: quarter notes, half notes, and dotted half notes.

Heaven

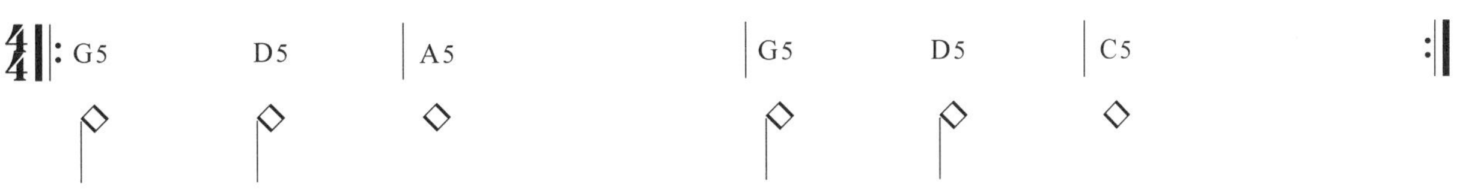

FIG. 2.15. "Heaven" Harmonic Rhythm

Watchtower

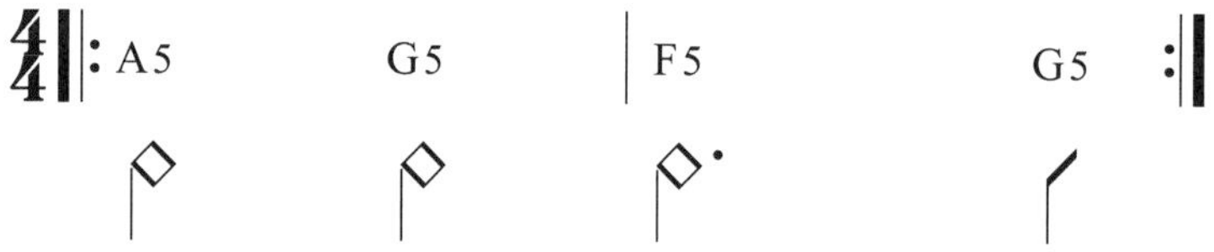

FIG. 2.16. "Watchtower" Harmonic Rhythm

The quarter note can be subdivided into two parts to create eighth notes, and into four parts to create sixteenth notes. The subdivisions are counted with the syllables in the chart. Practice counting these aloud with your metronome, and then playing them using power with the following charts.

Watchtower

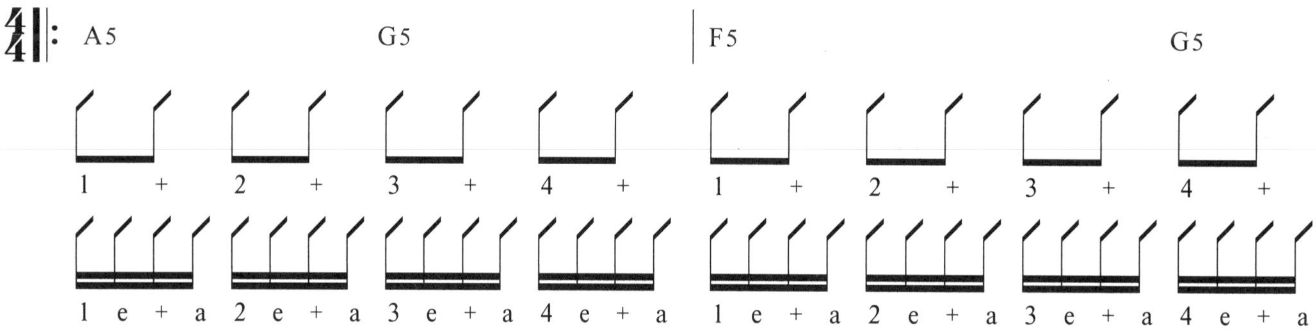

FIG. 2.17. "Watchtower" Subdivisions

Rest symbols indicate silence. There is a rest value that corresponds to every note value, and they are counted in the same way. Instead of writing in a whole rest, an entire measure of rest may be indicated with N.C. (No Chord). Sometimes, for rhythmic emphasis, a short note value is replaced by a quick, accented, percussive played note known as a "hit." In notation, the head of the "hit" note is replaced by an ×. In this excerpt of the song "Together," you'll read and play both a hit and an N.C.

Together

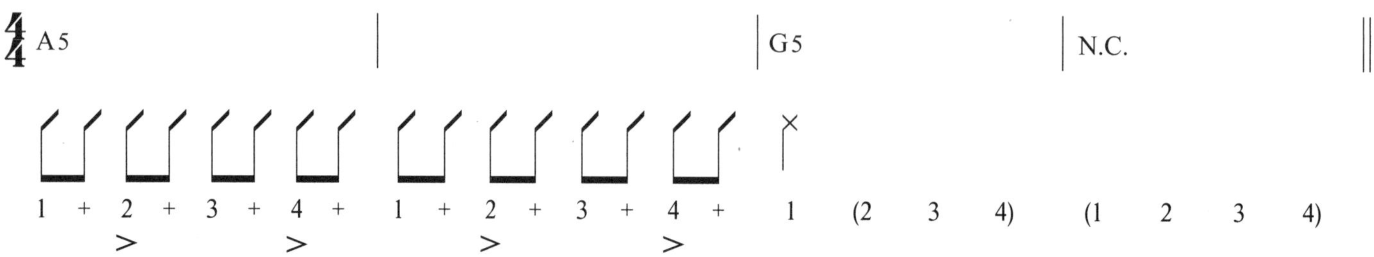

FIG. 2.18. Chart with Hit and N.C., "Together" (Excerpt)

A "tie" is a curved line that connects two notes with the same note name. You'll play the first note and hold it while counting the second. A tie is different from a rest because you'll let the note ring as you count instead of stopping the sound. The following chart, "People," uses the tie and places the chord change on the "+ of 2," creating a syncopated time feel that is a signature sound of R&B styles. To bring out this time feel, strum only on beat 1 and the "+ of 2." Use power chords to play through this chart.

People

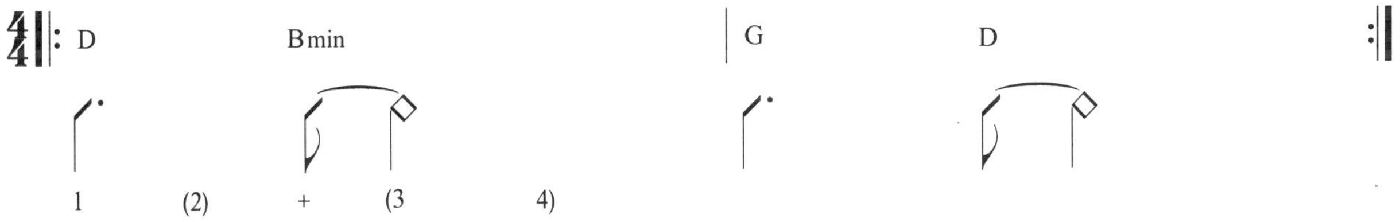

FIG. 2.19. Chart with a Tie and Dot, "People"

POWER CHORD STRUMMING PATTERNS

When rhythmic notation is not provided in a chart, you will play a strumming pattern of your choice. There are two common strumming patterns that you can learn and modify to fit the style and mood of the music: "split strum" and "straight eighths." Power chords favor down strums, meaning that you'll strum down in direction throughout.

Split Strum

In the split-strum pattern, beats 1 and 3 are strummed in eighth notes and beats 2 and 4 in quarter notes. This rhythmic pattern naturally brings out the backbeat groove.

Wisdom

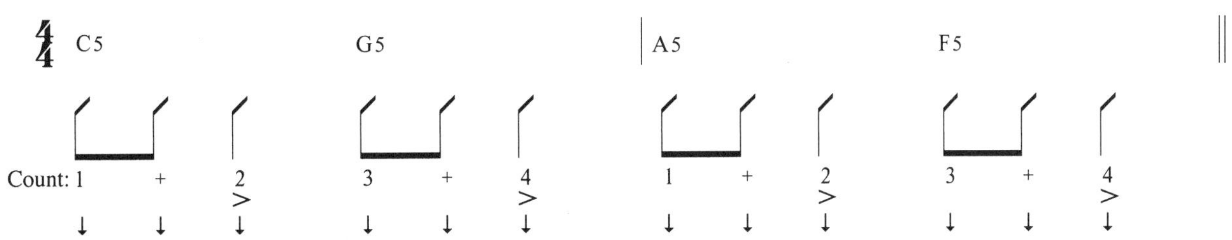

FIG. 2.20. Split-Strum Pattern, "Wisdom"

Straight Eighths

To strum in straight eighths, you'll strum the power chord on every eighth note. This is a common strumming pattern to hard rock styles.

Watchtower

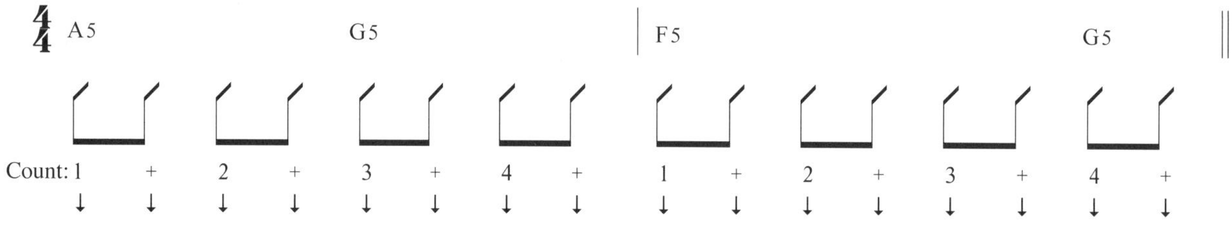

FIG. 2.21. Straight-Eighths Strumming Pattern, "Watchtower"

PRACTICE: CHART READING WITH POWER CHORDS

To work on your rhythm guitar parts, turn to the charts in part IV. For each chart, realize the chord symbols with power chords rooted on string ⑥. Play through the chart, working on the shifts between power chords until they are smooth. Next, choose a strumming pattern that fits the chart and practice it with the chord changes. Once you feel comfortable with these materials, turn on your metronome and practice the chart in time. Listen for clarity of tone, and enjoy the process of playing with different rhythms and strumming patterns.

CHAPTER 3

Lead Guitar Basics

The idea of "lead guitar" playing, "soloing," or "improvising" can be both exciting and intimidating. In its basic form, lead playing in popular and traditional music involves learning a scale pattern on the fretboard and varying the order, length, and sound of the notes to create melodies. In this chapter, we'll cover the materials and strategies to get you started. The scale we'll use to begin is called the "pentatonic scale."

PENTATONIC SCALE PATTERN 1

A pentatonic scale is a five-note scale used for improvisation in a variety of styles. There are different types of pentatonic scales, and we'll cover those common to popular music: the major and minor pentatonic scales. There are five fingering patterns for these pentatonic scales that connect on the fretboard. To begin, we'll work with the most common pattern for this scale, pattern 1. In chapter 5, we'll cover all five patterns (see figure 5.8).

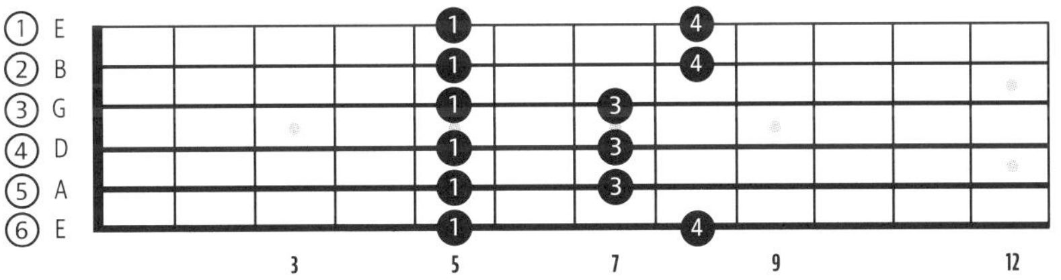

FIG. 3.1. Pentatonic Pattern 1

Pattern 1 is a "moveable pattern" that can be heard and used as either a minor pentatonic scale or a major pentatonic scale. You can set up the pattern on any root note on string ⑥, depending on the key in which you would like to play. We'll cover the music theory in chapter 5. For now, you'll start learning the pentatonic scale by playing.

To set up pentatonic scale pattern 1 as a minor pentatonic scale, fret your first finger on the root note on string ⑥, as shown. This example shows A minor pentatonic.

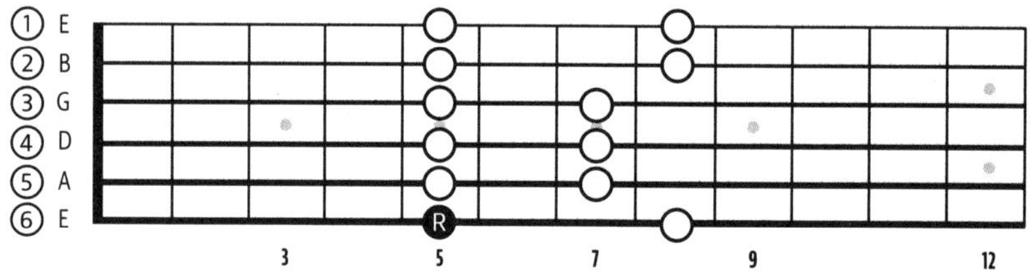

FIG. 3.2. Pentatonic Pattern 1 with Root on A for A Minor Pentatonic

To set up pentatonic scale pattern 1 as a major pentatonic scale, fret your fourth finger on the root note on string ⑥. This example shows C major pentatonic.

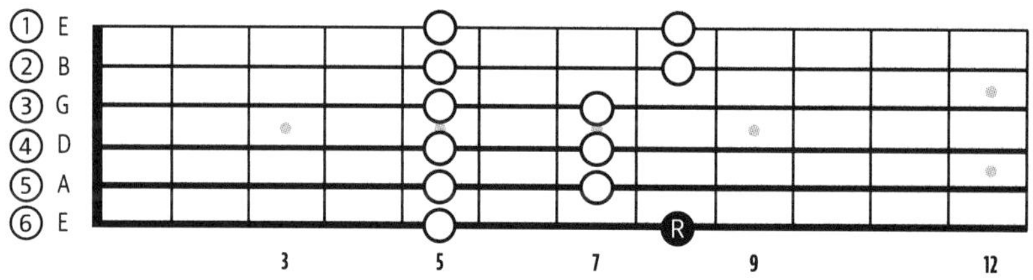

FIG. 3.3. Major Pentatonic with Root on C for C Major Pentatonic

PRACTICE: PENTATONIC PATTERNS

To practice the pentatonic pattern and become familiar with the setup for minor and major, follow these steps.

1. Fret pattern 1 as A minor pentatonic. Play through the pattern slowly, and listen to each note, ascending the scale, from strings ⑥ to ①. Alternate pick as you play.
2. Descend the scale in the same manner, from strings ① to ⑥.
3. Next, choose two strings in this pentatonic pattern. Play the notes included in the pattern on these two strings out of order. Then with only those notes, play a short musical idea about four or five notes in length. Vary the length and volume of each note as you play. Pause. Then answer your short, improvised idea with another. As you feel comfortable, add more notes from other strings in the pattern to your ideas.
4. Repeat this exercise, fretting pattern 1 as C major pentatonic, D minor pentatonic, and A major pentatonic.

SOLOING WITH THE PENTATONIC SCALE

To take a solo with the pentatonic scale in a chart, you'll develop the musical ideas you've been improvising into "phrases"—distinct melodies that follow the form of the song. Many popular songs are written in a form of two-bar or four-bar phrases. You might see this in the number of bars written in each line of a chart, and often hear it in the lyrics. At the end of each phrase in the lyrics, there might be a punctation mark, and a breath or pause. When you are improvising melodies that follow the phrase structure of the chart, add a rest in between each phrase.

To practice phrasing, start with the chart for "Wisdom." In the chart (figure 3.4), the two-bar phrase structure is indicated with phrase markings. In this exercise, you'll combine your rhythm guitar and lead guitar skills to create two parts.

1. Record the rhythm guitar part: use power chords and a strumming pattern of your choice, at your chosen tempo, playing in time with the metronome. Count four beats at the beginning of your recording, before you begin playing.
2. Prepare your lead guitar part: locate pentatonic pattern 1 in the designated key for the chart, C major pentatonic.
3. Play the recording of the rhythm guitar part. Listen to your four-beat count, and then begin to improvise.
4. Improvise a musical idea that follows the two-bar length of the first phrase marking. At the end, take a rest. At the beginning of the next phrase marking, answer your first phrase with a second. Continue to improvise through this chart in the same manner. You may repeat ideas and vary them as you'd like.
5. As you repeat this exercise, think about the form you are creating with your solo within the form of this chart. Are your melodic ideas ascending? Descending? Call and response? Repetitive? Contrasting? What forms could you try? What would happen if you varied the length of the phrases themselves?

Congratulations! Now, you are taking a solo!

Wisdom

4/4 |: C5 G5 | A5 F5 | C5 G5 | F5 C5 :|

FIG. 3.4. "Wisdom" with Phrase Markings

PRACTICE: LEAD PLAYING WITH CHARTS

Deepen your work with the charts in part IV by strengthening your rhythm guitar playing and developing your phrasing in improvisation. In your rhythm parts, use power chords rooted on strings ⑥ and ⑤. For the lead part, the practice notes introducing each chart will guide you to the appropriate pentatonic scale pattern. Note the chart structure, and match the phrasing to that layout in your solo. Use your phrases to build a story as you improvise!

CHAPTER 4

Reading Basics

Reading and writing standard notation is useful when playing with other instrumentalists, and knowing tab gives you a shorthand to use with fellow guitarists. Reading fluently on the guitar is a skill you'll develop over time. This chapter is a notation overview to get you started. The *Modern Method for Guitar* series by William Leavitt (Berklee Press) is an excellent resource for further developing your reading skills on the guitar.

NOTES ON THE FRETBOARD

The first step in learning how to read notated music on the guitar is to become familiar with all note locations on the fretboard. In previous chapters, you learned the notes on strings ⑥ and ⑤. Now, take a look at the notes on strings ④ to ①. Practice locating and naming these notes.

String ⑥

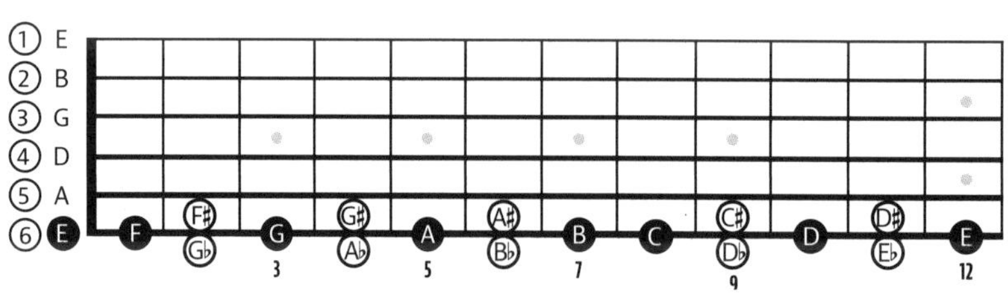

String ⑤

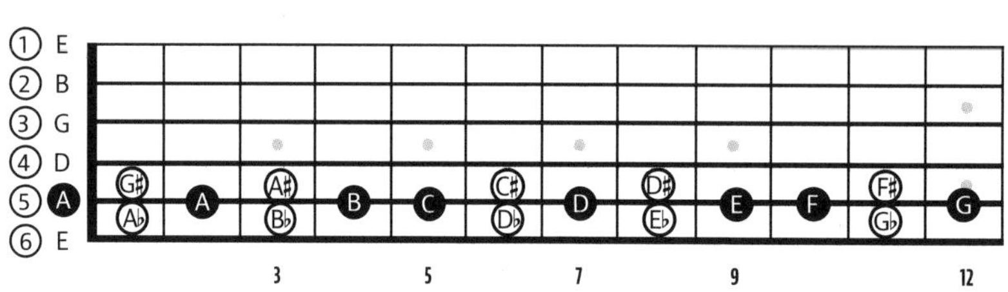

String ④

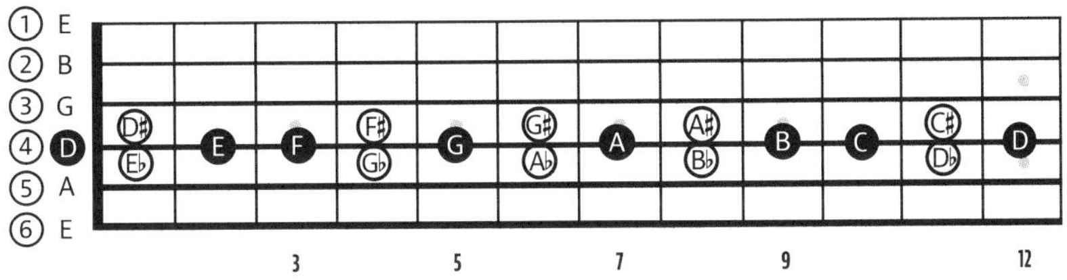

String ③

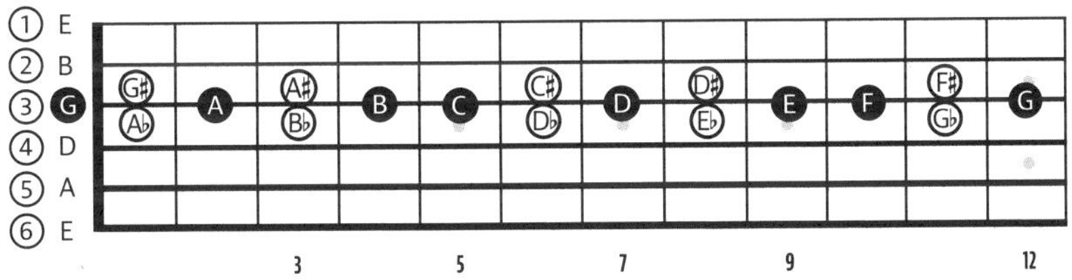

String ②

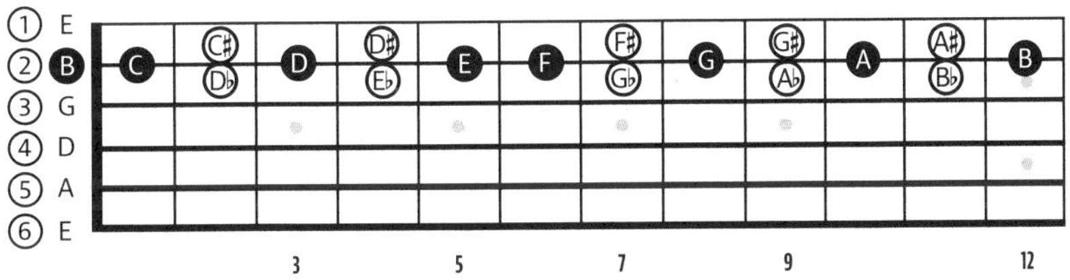

String ①

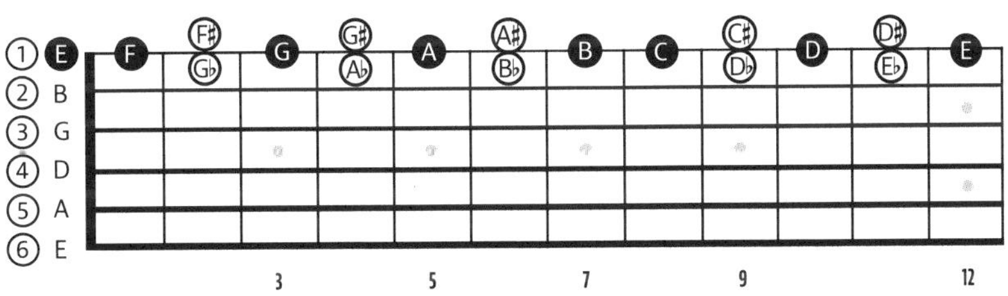

FIG. 4.1. Notes on Each String

NATURAL NOTES

Practicing the natural notes is a great way to map the fretboard.

1. Play the natural notes slowly up and down one string at a time. Play them in and out of order, naming them and memorizing their location.
2. Next, improvise melodies on one string at a time, using only natural notes.

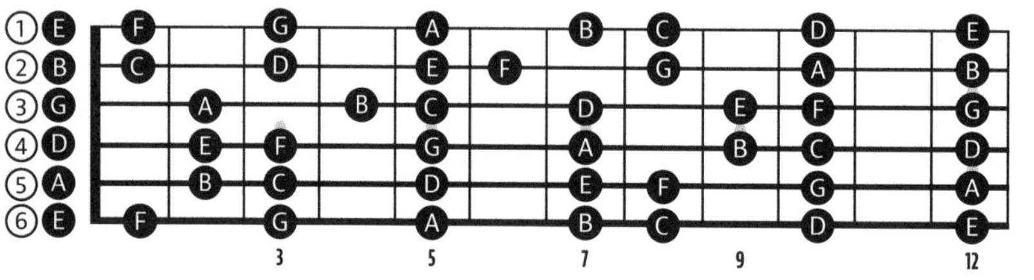

FIG. 4.2. Natural Notes on the Fretboard

3. Then, choose one note, "C" for example, and find it on every string.

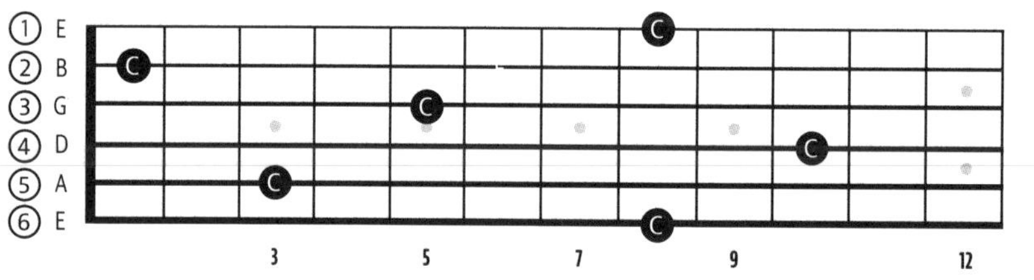

FIG. 4.3. Note C Across the Neck on All Strings

STANDARD NOTATION BASICS

In standard notation, music for guitar is notated in the treble clef. The guitar is a "transposing instrument" by one octave, meaning that the notes will sound one octave lower than written. In figure 4.4, the five lines make up the "staff." On the left-hand side, you'll see the treble clef symbol, which indicates that the notation can be read on guitar. The time signature indicates the way in which to count the notes.

Notes appear either on the lines or spaces of the staff. You may have heard some catchy sayings to help you remember the names of the lines and spaces. The lines from the bottom to top are often remembered by: "**E**very **G**irl **B**and **D**eserves **F**unding," and the spaces from the bottom up spell "**FACE**."

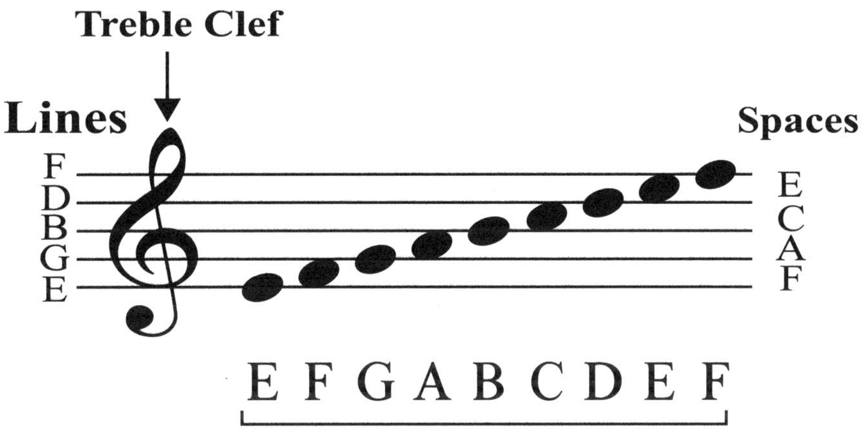

FIG. 4.4. Staff Lines and Spaces

Notes that fall below and above the staff are written on "ledger lines" and "spaces" that extend the staff. Some of the notes on string ⑥ and ⑤ use ledger lines below the staff, and some of the notes on the higher strings, up the neck, use ledger lines above the staff.

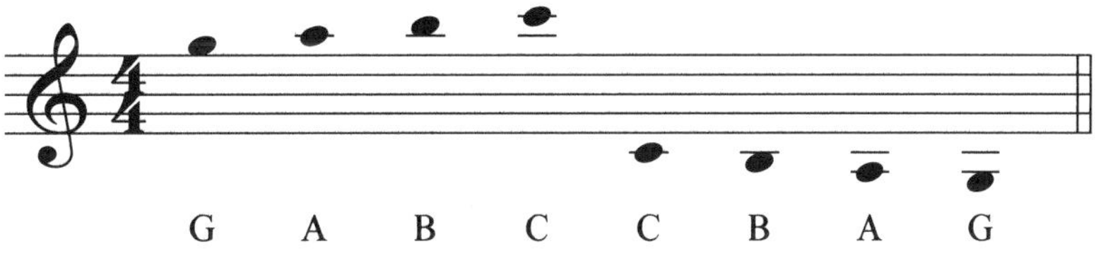

FIG. 4.5. Ledger Lines

Rhythmic Values in Standard Notation

In standard notation, notes are written with a note head and a rhythmic value that shows you the note's duration. In chapter 2, you learned the basic rhythmic values that allow you to write and read rhythms "in four." The following example, "Acceptance," is a notated melody notated with rhythmic values.

FIG. 4.6. Notated Melody, "Acceptance"

READING STANDARD NOTATION IN 1ST POSITION

Reading standard notation on the guitar is like meeting a new person. You need to know their name (note name), where they are located (on the fretboard), and what they look like (on the staff). As the same person might be at home in multiple places, some notes will be found in more than one location on the neck.

On the guitar, written music is read "in position." A position is determined by the location of your first finger on the fretboard, and includes the frets your other fingers can reach without shifting. In this book, you'll practice reading the notes in 1st and 5th positions. Later in your study, you'll expand your reading to 7th and 10th positions.

The first step in reading in 1st position is to familiarize yourself with the notes in that position. Set up your fretting hand with your first finger at the 1st fret of string ⑥. Play through the natural notes across all six strings, naming the notes of the musical alphabet as you play each one.

NATURAL NOTES IN THE 1ST POSITION

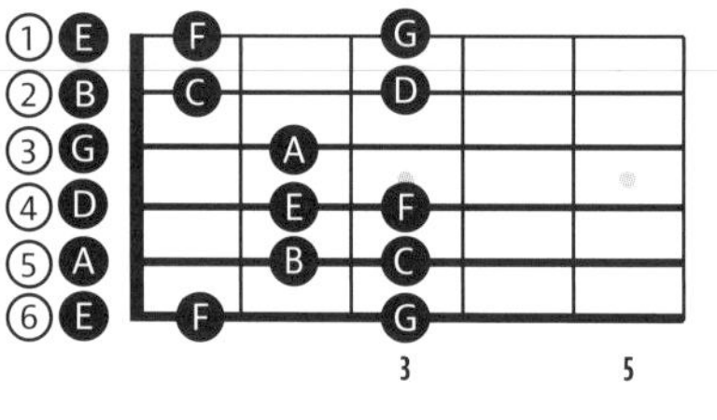

FIG. 4.7. Natural Notes 1st Position

Figure 4.8 shows the notes in the 1st position on the staff, with fret numbers marked.

FIG. 4.8. Staff Notation, Notes in 1st Position

PRACTICE: READING MELODIES IN 1ST POSITION

Practice reading the five melodies in figure 4.9, composed with natural notes in 1st position. Note that the numbers under the notes indicate the fretting-hand fingerings.

1. First, focus on the noteheads and note names alone, locating them and playing them on the fretboard. Say the note names aloud as you play.
2. Next, put your guitar aside. Using your metronome, count through the rhythms, using the rhythm syllables from the chart in chapter 2, figure 2.14.
3. Finally, combine the note names and locations with the rhythms by playing the notes of each example and counting the rhythms.

Deepen your practice by writing your own melodies to read! You may improvise in 1st position and notate your improvisations, or write first.

Natural Notes on ⑥⑤

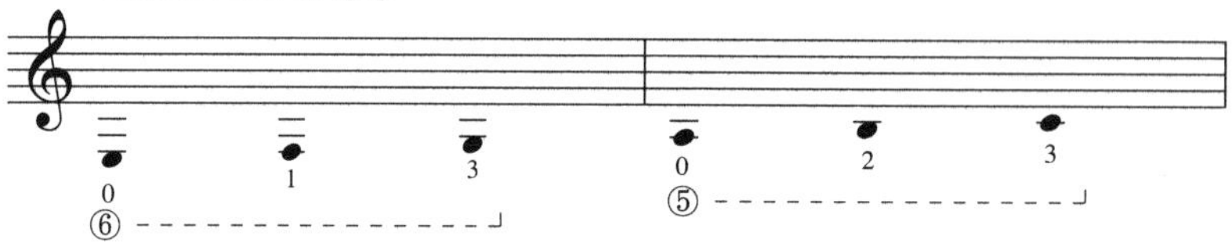

Melody 1

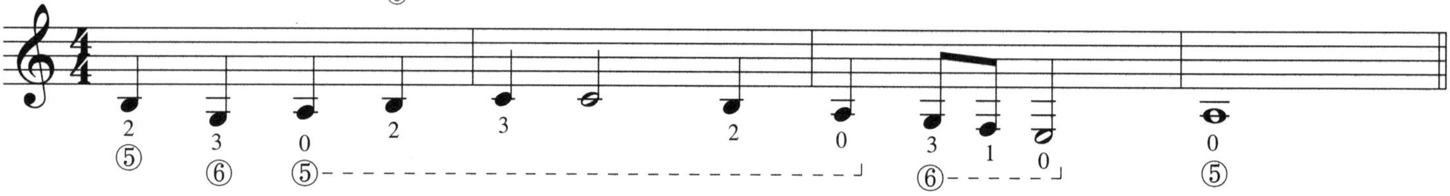

Natural Notes on ④③

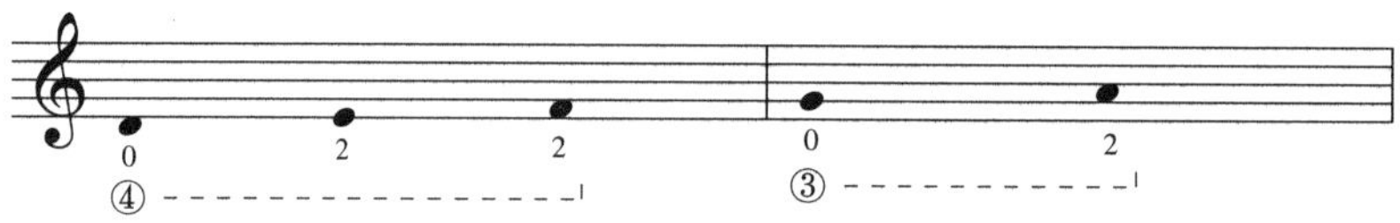

Melody 2

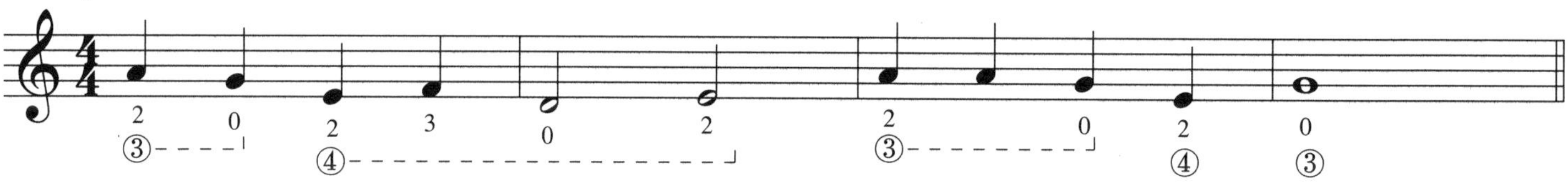

Natural Notes on ②①

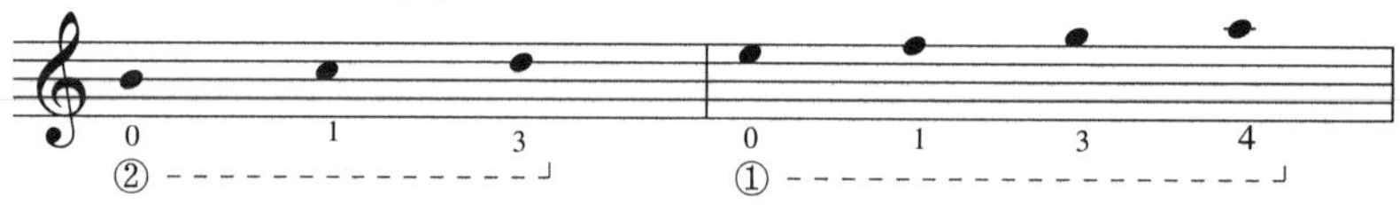

Melody 3

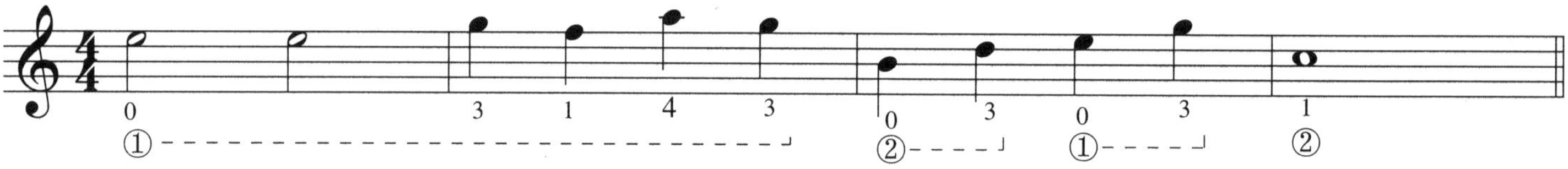

MIXED STRING MELODIES WITH SHARPS AND FLATS

Melody 4

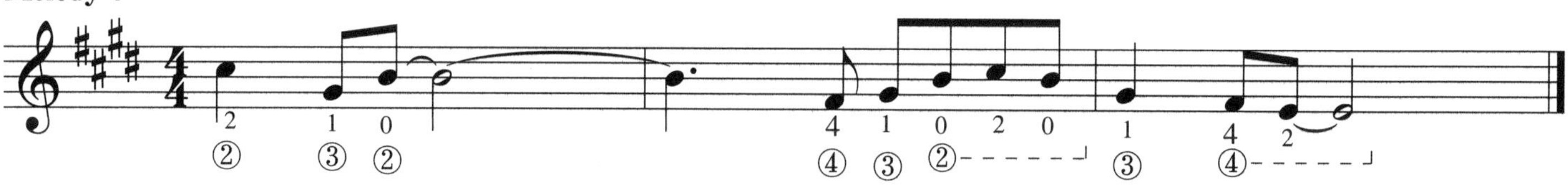

Melody 5

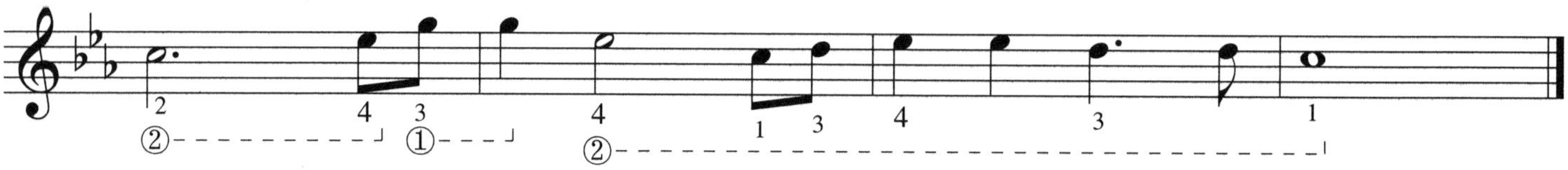

FIG. 4.9. Reading Practice, 1st Position

READING STANDARD NOTATION IN 5TH POSITION

To locate the natural notes in 5th position, shift your first finger to the 5th fret on string ⑥. First, learn the notes across the 5th fret: ⑥ = A, ⑤ = D, ④ = G, ③ = C, ② = E, ① = A

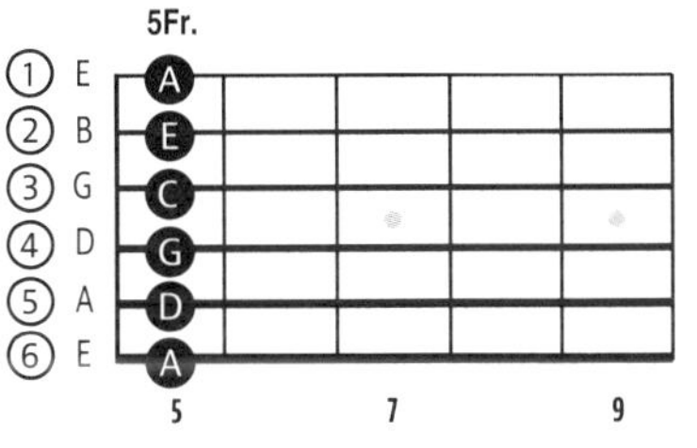

FIG. 4.10. Notes Across the 5th Fret

Starting with the A on string ⑥, play and name the natural notes in the 5th position. Notice that you have played most of these notes when you played pentatonic pattern 1 in the keys of A minor and C major! Playing in 5th position provides access to higher notes, and lends a darker tone color to the same notes you've been playing in 1st position.

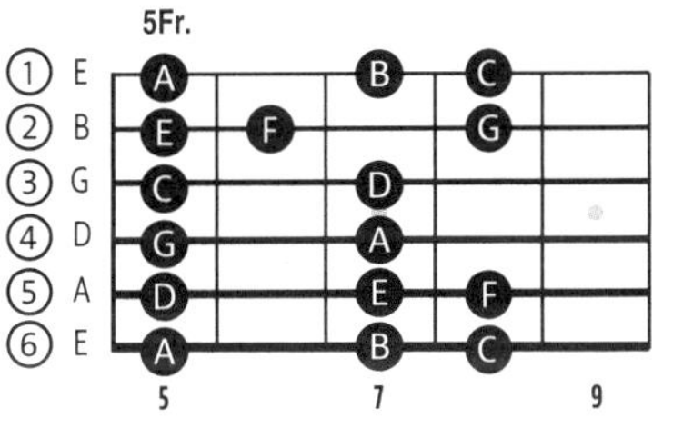

FIG. 4.11. Natural Notes in 5th Position

Now, look at chart 4.12, which shows the notation for the notes in 5th position. Play through the notes on each string again, memorizing the notation for each note.

FIG. 4.12. Notes in 5th Position

PRACTICE: READING MELODIES IN 5TH POSITION

Practice reading the following examples in the 5th position. Follow the steps you used to work with the examples in the 1st position. Here, small numbers refer to fingerings, not frets.

Strings ⑥ and ⑤

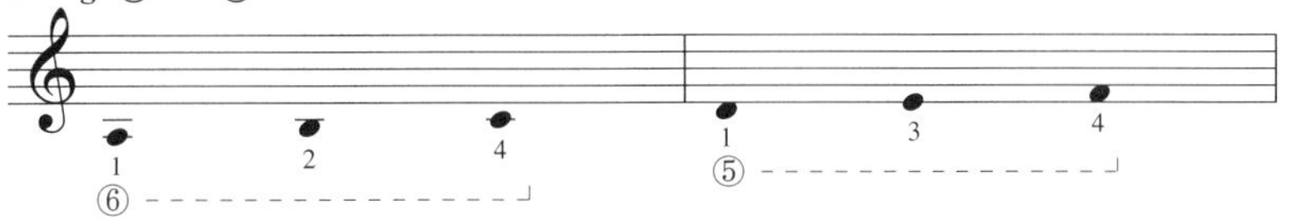

Reading Example 1: 5th Position, Strings ⑥ and ⑤

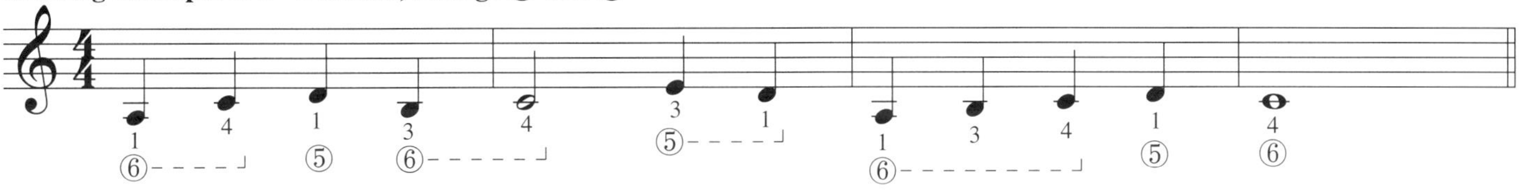

Strings ④ and ③

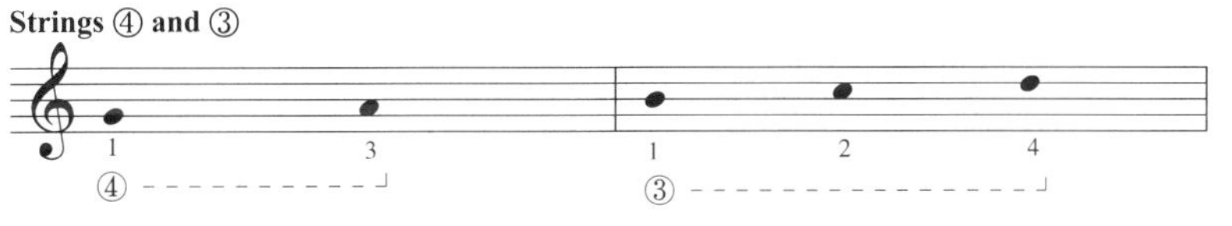

Reading Example 2: 5th Position, Strings ④ and ③

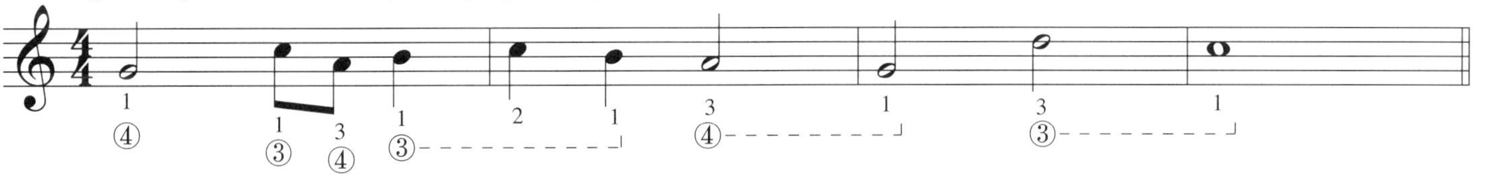

Strings ② and ①

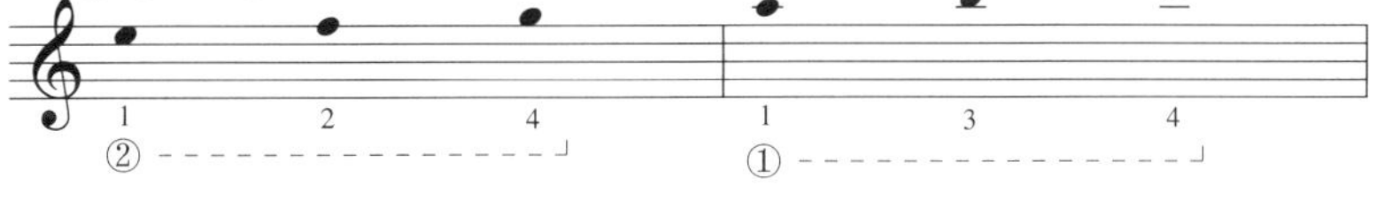

Reading Example 3: 5th Position, Strings ② and ①

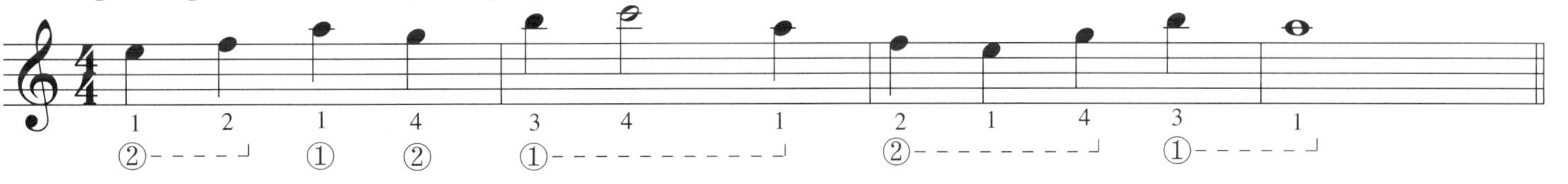

Reading Example 4: 5th Position, Strings ⑥ to ①

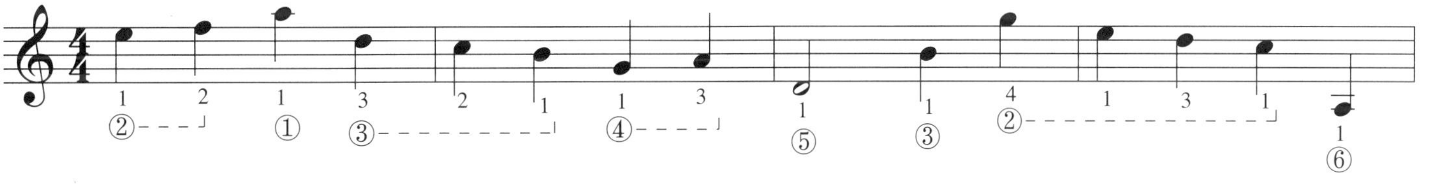

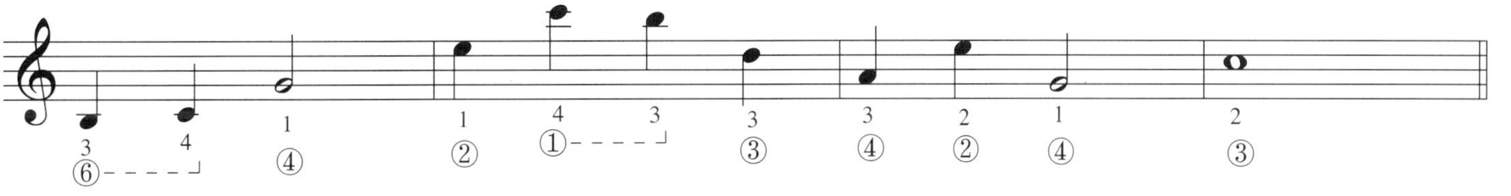

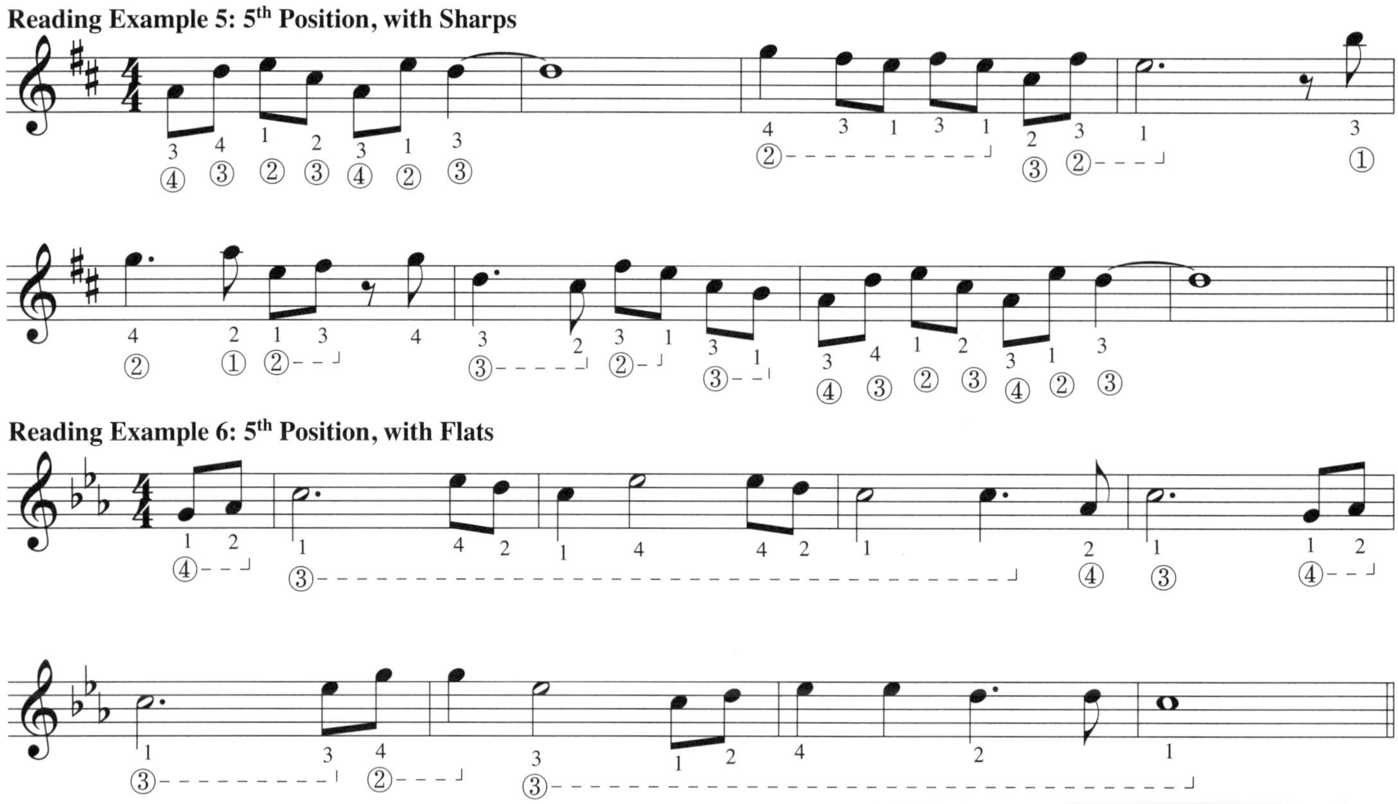

FIG. 4.13. Reading Practice, 5th Position

READING IN 1ST AND 5TH POSITIONS: "TAKING THE TOUR"

Take one short melody "on a tour" of the 1st and 5th positions by reading it in both. Next, improvise melodies in 1st position, and notate them on a piece of staff paper. Take your own melodies on a reading tour of 1st and 5th positions.

FIG. 4.14. Notated "Acceptance" Melody in 1st and 5th Positions

READING TAB

"Tab" is short for "tablature"—melodic notation used for fretted string instruments. In guitar tablature, the six lines represent the six guitar strings. The bottom line represents string ⑥. The numbers on each line represent the frets played on each string. Rhythmic notation may be added above or below the tablature.

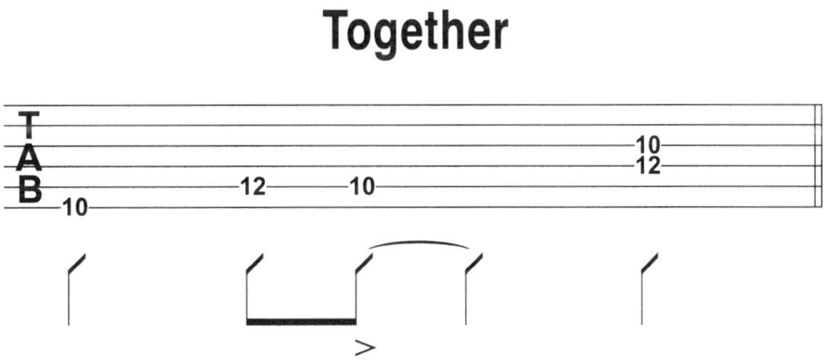

FIG. 4.15. Tab Example, "Together" Melody

While tab is an effective guitar notation, it does not allow for a guitarist to make position changes. The fretboard location of the notes is set by the notation itself. Take a look at the figure 4.16 "Acceptance" melody, "on tour" of 1st and 5th positions, notated with both standard notation and tab.

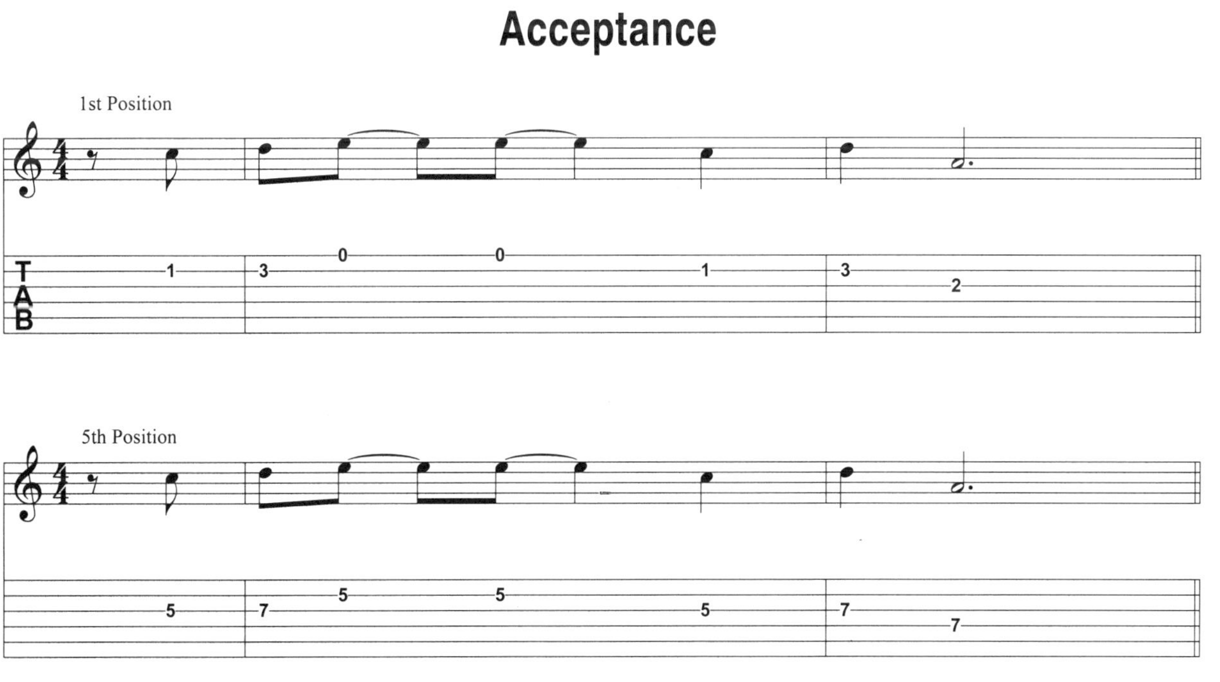

FIG. 4.16. "Acceptance" Melody, with Tab for 1st and 5th Positions

READING AND NOTATING RIFFS

A "riff" is a short, distinctive melody, often played in a low register, and commonly notated in tab. Notice that the notes in the "Sea" riff are played in pattern 1 of A minor pentatonic. Read this riff. Then, improvise your own riff, using the same pentatonic pattern, and notate your riff in tab.

Sea

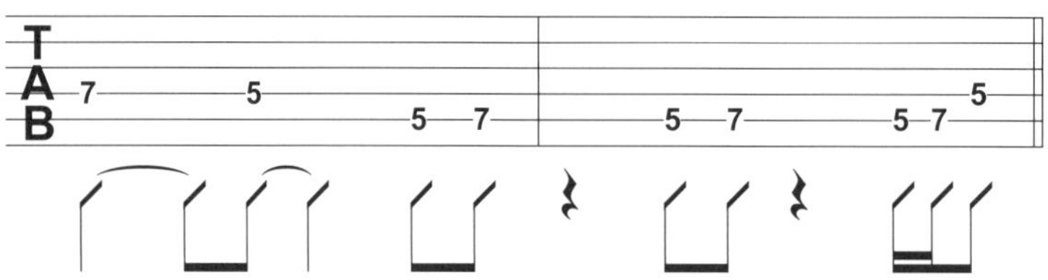

FIG. 4.17. "Sea" Riff Written in Tab

PRACTICE: NOTATION IN CHARTS

In part IV, some of the charts include standard notation and tab. After working through the reading examples in this chapter, take a look at a few common ways in which notation is used in those longer song charts. Practice the melodies in each chart until they sound spontaneous and fluid. Then, work these learned melodies into your lead guitar part in your arrangement.

PART I REVIEW

At this point in your study, you've established a solid foundation of guitar basics. You'll deepen your knowledge of these materials, techniques, and concepts in your practice and in your chart reading. In your practice, take time to review the topics from the part I chapters: Check on your posture, hand positions, basic techniques. Rotate your work with the notes on the fretboard, power chords, rhythmic groove and notation, improvising and phrasing with the pentatonic pattern, and reading notation.

Enjoy each moment as you strengthening your guitar foundation. Remember to breathe!

Part II

Building on the Basics

Now that you are playing charts with rhythm and lead guitar parts and becoming familiar with the fretboard, it's time to build on your foundation by adding options to your toolbox and depth to your musicianship. The chapters in part II introduce the music theory behind scales and chords, additional scale and chord forms, and strategies for improvisation and strumming that will take your playing to the next level.

We'll start in chapter 5 by working through scale patterns that will expand your soloing on the fretboard and the music theory for ear training. Chapters 6 and 7 introduce the common open chord shapes, strumming patterns, and the theory behind the sounds many hit songs have in common. In chapter 8, you'll work on the basics of fingerstyle technique for accompaniment patterns that set a foundation for solo arrangements.

While you work through part II, you'll likely see some familiar materials and find a few surprises. As usual, take it slow, and enjoy the moments of recognition and discovery.

CHAPTER 5

Lead Guitar Expansion

Now that you've improvised with pattern 1 of the pentatonic, it's time to go deeper into the music theory behind that scale, and learn all five fingering patterns on the fretboard. The music theory will help you organize the fretboard and strengthen your ear. The five patterns of the pentatonic scale will provide exciting options for your soloing and writing.

SCALE THEORY: MAJOR

The five-note pentatonic scales that you've been playing so far in this book are derived from the major scale. The major scale is an arrangement of the seven notes of the musical alphabet in which there is a half-step between the third and fourth notes and the seventh and first notes, and a whole step between every other pair of notes. When the musical alphabet begins on the note C, this pattern occurs naturally. The natural half steps, E–F and B–C, fall between the third/fourth and seventh/first (octave) notes of the scale. In a scale, the numbered notes are called "scale degrees."

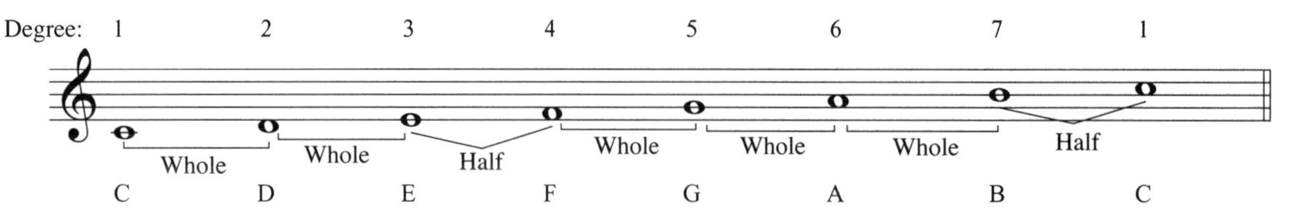

FIG. 5.1. C Major Scale, with Whole and Half Steps Marked

This whole step/half step pattern must be maintained in the major scale. When the major scale begins on a note other than C, sharps and flats are used to create whole steps and half steps where they do not naturally occur.

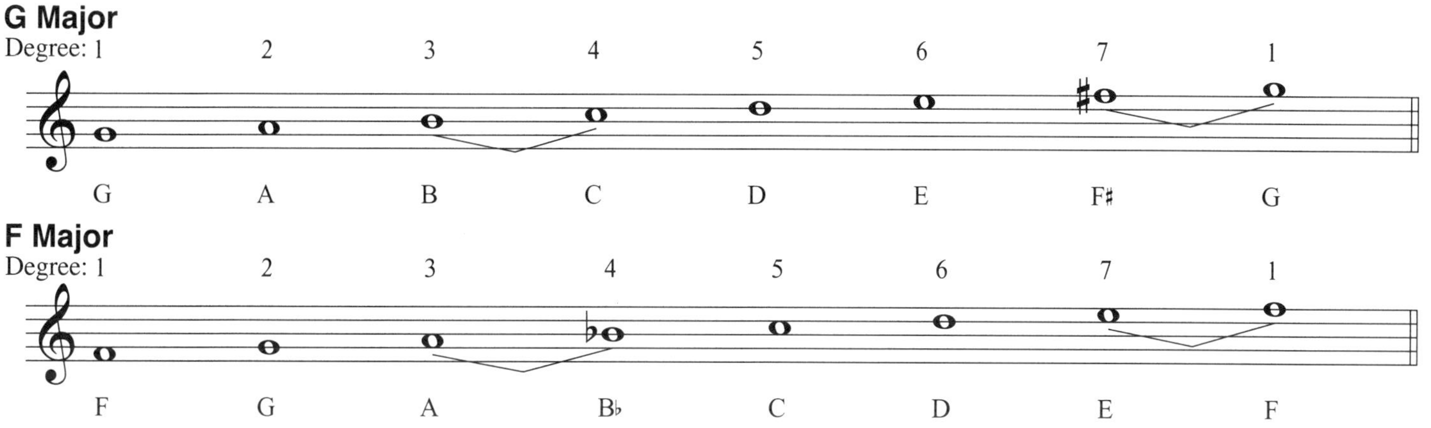

FIG. 5.2. G Major and F Major Scales

When a composer is writing in a particular scale that requires a sharp or flat, they'll often put it in the "key signature." A key signature is a collection of the sharps or flats required for the scale, located right after the clef and just before the time signature in standard notation. This indicates which notes are altered each time they are played. In figure 5.3, for example, you'll "sharp" any notes F and C.

FIG. 5.3. Key Signature Example, "People" Melody

SCALE THEORY: PENTATONIC

The major and minor pentatonic scales you played earlier in this book are derived from the major scale. Literally, pentatonic means "five notes." The major pentatonic scale contains five notes, or "degrees," of the major scale. The minor pentatonic also contains five degrees of the major scale but with two alterations.

The major pentatonic scale contains degrees 1 2 3 5 6 of the major scale.

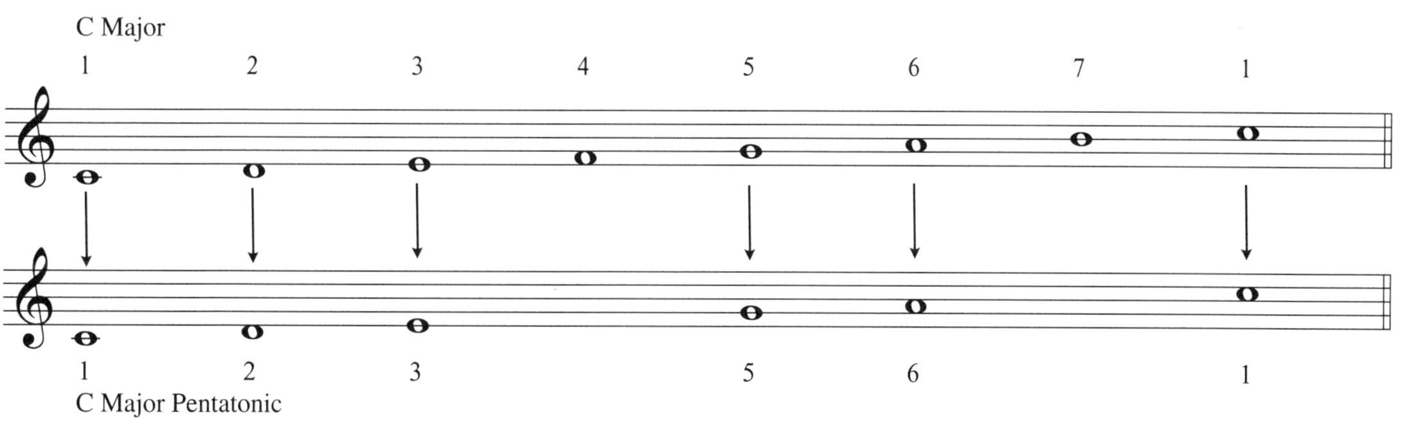

FIG. 5.4. C Major Pentatonic Derived from Major

Minor pentatonic contains degrees 1 ♭3 4 5 ♭7 of the major scale. This means that you lower (flat) the notes on the third and seventh degrees of the major scale by one half step to create the minor pentatonic.

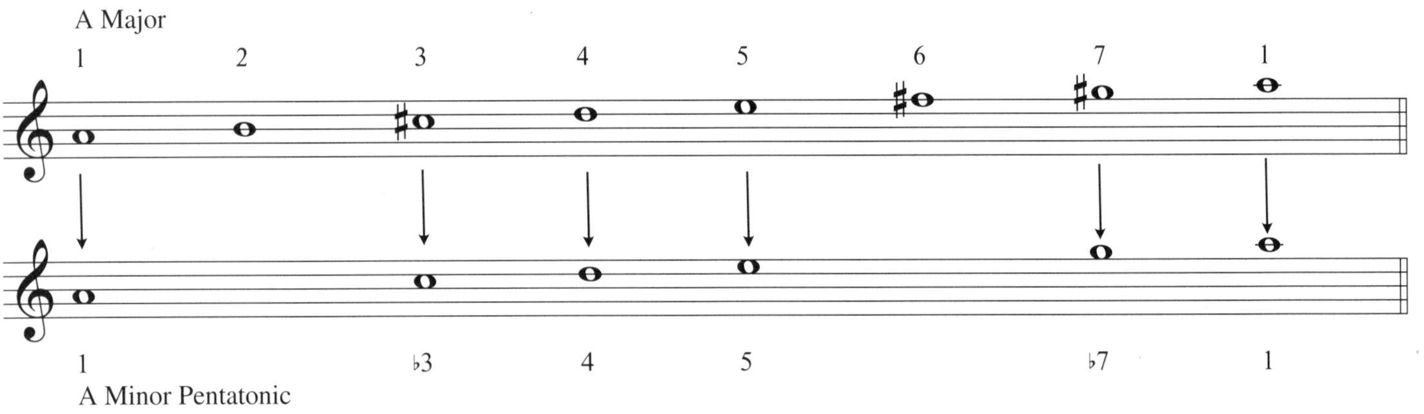

FIG. 5.5. A Minor Pentatonic Derived from Major

Notice that the notes of the C major pentatonic and the A minor pentatonic are the same! This is why you play them with the same pentatonic fingering pattern. The difference in the way you will hear and use the C major and A minor pentatonic will depend on which note, C or A, is your sonic home base. We'll explore this concept of "relative" scales further in chapter 9.

The notes of a scale in a melody are often named by their scale degrees. For example, if I wrote a melody in C major pentatonic with the notes E, D, and C, I may tell you to play "3-2-1." This way, you would be able to play it in C major pentatonic, or you could play it in another key. For example, 3-2-1 in D major pentatonic would be the notes: F♯, E, and D. With practice, your ear will begin to recognize the pattern of the major scale degree numbers in a melody no matter the key. This is how musicians "play by ear." The practice of playing a melody with the same scale degree numbers in different keys is called "transposition." You'll do this on the guitar by changing the location of your pentatonic scale pattern on the fretboard.

PRACTICE: RIFF WRITING AND EAR TRAINING

The scale degrees numbers that make up these major and minor pentatonic scale patterns can be used to write melodies/riffs and for ear training. First, we'll work with minor pentatonic and then with major pentatonic. To begin, we will use fret pentatonic pattern 1 in A minor. Play the pattern, naming the note names and scale degree numbers for each note: A = 1, C = ♭3, D = 4, E = 5, G = ♭7, using the diagram in figure 5.7 for reference.

Write out a short group of these scale degree numbers, in an order of your choosing. Play what you've written in the pattern 1, singing the scale degrees as you play, to train your ear. Then, move pentatonic pattern 1 to new minor key, and repeat these steps.

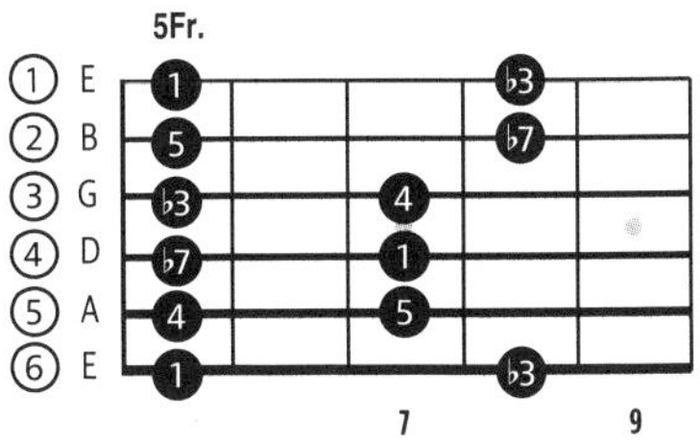

FIG. 5.6. A Minor Pentatonic Scale Degrees in 5th Position

Remember the "Sea" riff from chapter 4, figure 4.17? Here it is, written in scale degrees. Note that rhythmic notation is not included scale degree notation. This means that you can play the original riff and also create your own by varying the note durations.

1	♭7	4	5	4	5	4	5	♭7
④	⑤							④

Next, work with the scale degrees of the major pentatonic, using the same steps you went through with the minor pentatonic.

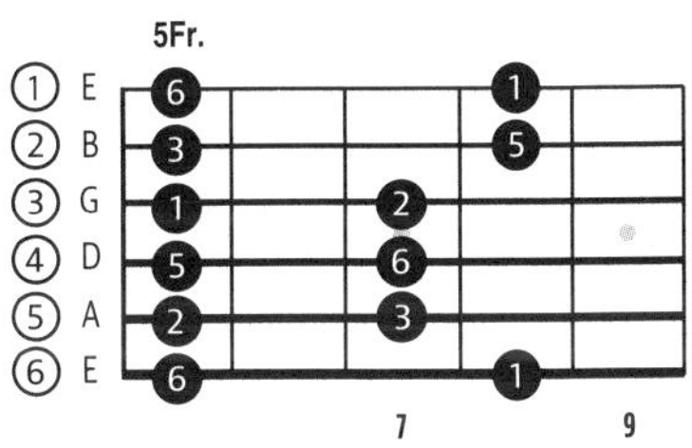

FIG. 5.7. C Major Pentatonic Scale Degrees

Review the "Acceptance" melody from chapter 4, figure 4.16. Play the original melody, and create your own variations by altering the rhythms.

1	2	3	3	1	2	6
③		②		③		④

SCALE PATTERNS: FIVE PATTERNS OF THE PENTATONIC SCALE

There are five fingering patterns for the pentatonic: one that begins on each note of the scale. The following diagrams show all five patterns, fretted in the keys of A minor and C major, with the scale degrees indicated. Note that each pattern overlaps with the next on the fretboard. This will allow you to ascend and descend as you improvise by connecting the patterns. To change keys, set your hand up on the intended root note in each pattern.

Pentatonic Pattern	A Minor	C Major
5	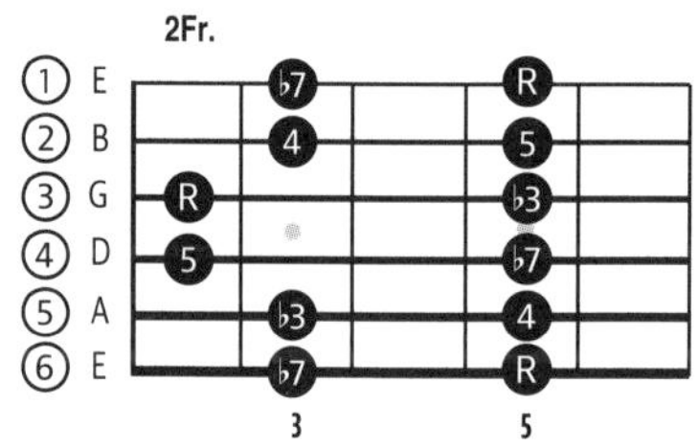	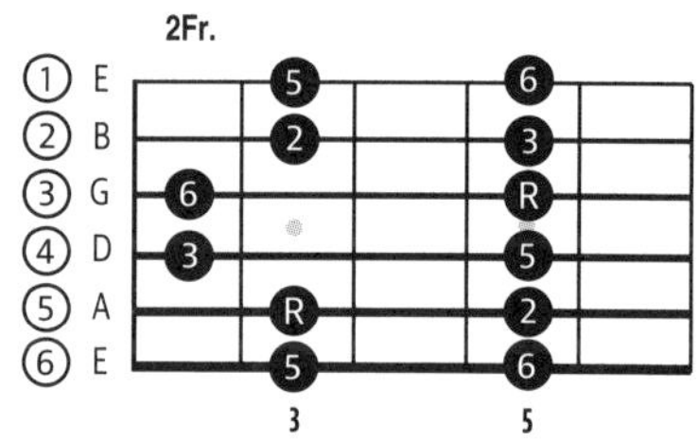
1	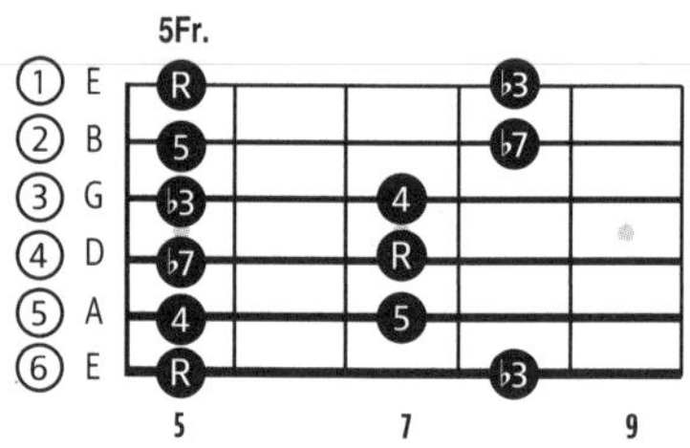	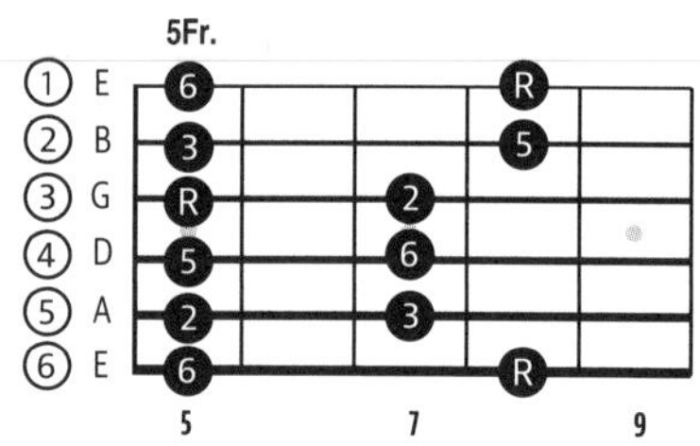
2	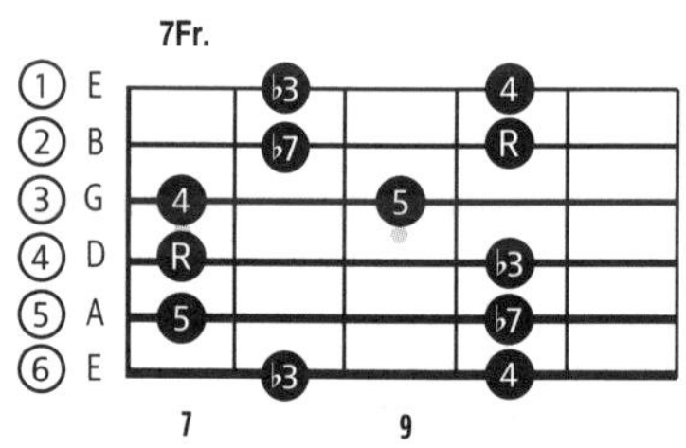	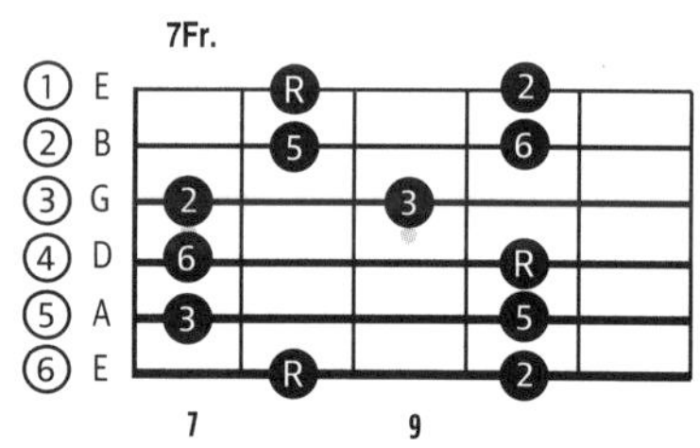
3	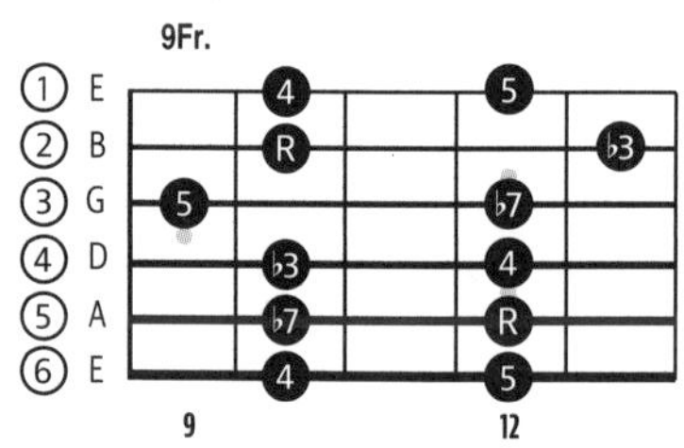	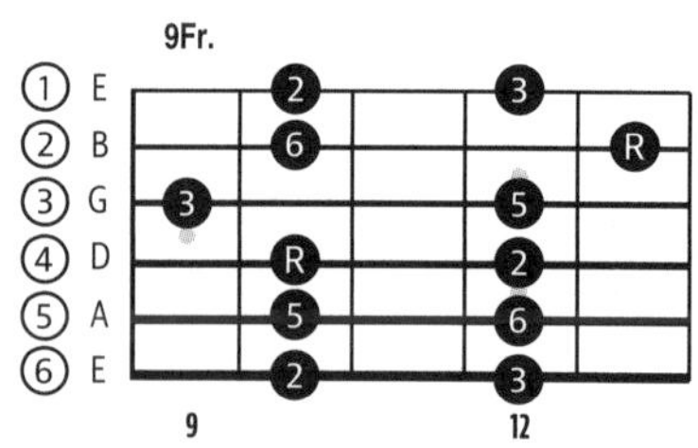
4	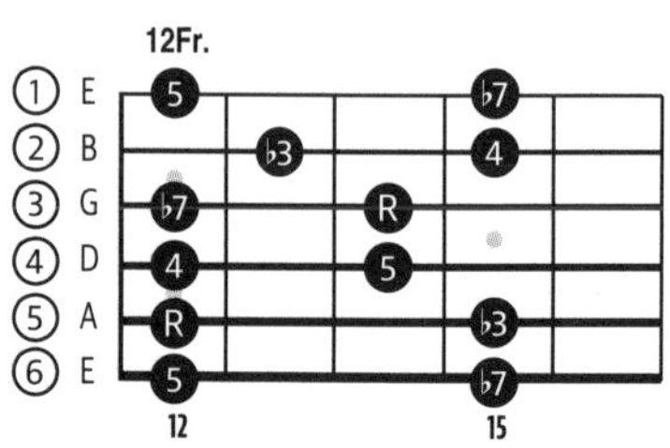	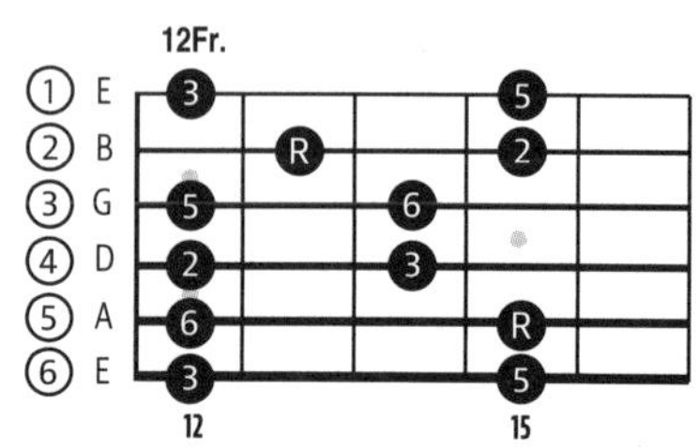

FIG. 5.8. Pentatonic Patterns 1, 2, 3, 4, 5. Major and Minor with Scale Degrees.

CONNECTING PENTATONIC PATTERNS

The first step in connecting multiple pentatonic patterns in improvisation is to work thoroughly with each. Practice each pattern slowly, in time, with awareness of technique and tone, while singing the scale degree numbers. Be creative, improvising melodies and soloing with these patterns in our song charts. Once you're comfortable with two adjacent patterns, practice connecting them by following these steps:

1. Begin in the lower pattern, ascending from string ⑥ to ①.
2. Shift up into the higher pattern on string ①.
3. Descend in the higher pattern, and shift back to the lower pattern on string ⑥. Repeat this process several times, each time shifting between the two patterns on different strings.
4. Now, improvise melodies using these two patterns. Note the lyrical and tonal possibilities that open up when you connect the patterns!
5. As you feel comfortable, repeat this exercise with each pair of adjacent patterns—connecting more than two. Remember, the more thoroughly you practice all aspects of the fingerings and the theory, the more fluid your improvisation will become.

TECHNIQUES FOR TONE: PARAMETERS OF SOUND

To develop a personal sound while improvising, you'll work on your tone: the volume, shape, and color of the notes you play. These parameters of sound are aspects of tone production that each have a technical approach to practice.

"Dynamics" refers to the volume level of a note. The following symbols correspond to volume levels: ***p*** = soft, ***mf*** = medium loud, ***f*** = loud.

Dynamic levels are dependent on weight. The more you push into the string as you are playing with your finger, the louder your dynamic level will be. As you practice establishing three distinct dynamic levels, do not confuse weight with force, or "hitting the string harder." Using force instead of weight will add an accent to the note instead of adjusting the dynamic level.

"Timbre" refers to the color of a note. For a brighter sound, move your picking hand close to the bridge to play a note. For a darker sound, move your picking hand towards the neck. As you practice this, pay attention to your hand placement and the corresponding timbre of the note you are playing.

"Envelope" refers to the sonic shape of a note. To begin your work with envelope, answer these questions about the attack, sustain, and release of the notes. Are you hitting the note with force or playing it with a gentle fluid motion? Are you playing all of the notes in a melody with the same attack? If they are varied, is this intentional? Are you playing the notes short in length with a space between notes in succession, or holding onto them as long as you can, connecting notes in your melodies?

Each of the parameters of sound is affected by your level of relaxation and technique as you play. As you practice each parameter, take a moment to consider your fretting-hand and picking-hand posture and technique. Remember to breathe!

PRACTICE: "THE ONE NOTE SOLO"

"The One Note Solo" is an exercise designed to help you practice the parameters of sound. Record the rhythm guitar part for one of the charts in part IV, referenced in the practice section. Choose one note in one pattern of the indicated pentatonic. Improvise a guitar solo using only that one note, the parameters of sound, rhythms, and phrasing. Now, dynamics, timbre, and envelope are your only tools for expression!

PRACTICE: SOLOING WITH PENTATONICS

Play the charts in part IV, and work on your improvisation with your own recorded rhythm track or with a partner. Now, you know there is a world of possibility for your practice! Improvise a series of melodic phrases: Start with the "one-note solo," incorporate learned and composed riffs, and improvise melodic phrases with pentatonic patterns of your choice. Practice different fingering pathways to connect the patterns on the fretboard. Take a moment to notate your favorite improvisations in standard notation and tab. Identify the scale degrees in your melodies, and sing them. Develop your awareness and control of the parameters of sound. Record your solos, and listen back to your phrasing and time.

With this type of practice, you are truly expanding your lead guitar playing!

CHAPTER 6

Rhythm Guitar Expansion

So far in this book, power chords have been our main tool for rhythm guitar playing. In this chapter, we'll add "open chords," commonly referred to as "folk chords" or "cowboy chords." We'll take a look at the familiar open chord shapes in useful groups for chart reading and technical practice, and cover common strumming patterns.

OPEN CHORDS

Open chords are fretted with recognizable chord shapes, and played in first position. They are called "open" chords because, in most cases, one or more open strings in the chord shape rings. Open chords can be used to realize chord symbols in a chart. In chapter 7, we'll explore the music theory of chord construction. For now, you'll memorize the chord names and the shorthand in their symbols:

- Major chords are indicated with capital letters: D.
- Minor chords are indicated with a capital letter followed by min: Dmin.
- Dominant 7 chords are indicated with a capital letter and a number 7: D7.
- Minor 7 chords are indicated with a capital letter, a "min," and a number 7: Dmin7.

Open Chords, Group 1

To start working with open chords, you'll learn the fingering shapes for nine common chords: C, F, D, G, Amin, Dmin, Emin, Amin7, D7. Because most songs use three or four chords, you'll group them in your practice in preparation. Begin with the groupings from our practice charts in part 1, and try one new group.

- Wisdom: C, G, Amin, F
- Heaven: G, D, Amin; G, D, C
- Watchtower: Amin, G, F, G
- New Group 1: G, Emin, C, D7, G
- New Group 2: C, Dmin, F, C

As you practice, isolate and memorize each individual shape. Make the shape with your fretting hand, and use the weight of your arm to assist you in depressing the strings. Your thumb should work to balance, rather than press into the back of the guitar neck. Strum the indicated strings, with the goal of creating a clear sound. To work on the chord changes, choose two chords from the group, and practice shifting from shape to shape. Move slowly, noting common notes between shapes. When there are no common fingers, make the next shape in the air as you are shifting. Repeat this process until your shifts are smooth and the chords sound clear when you strum each one. Some shapes will come easily, and others will take longer to fret with ease. Take your time, and remember to breathe!

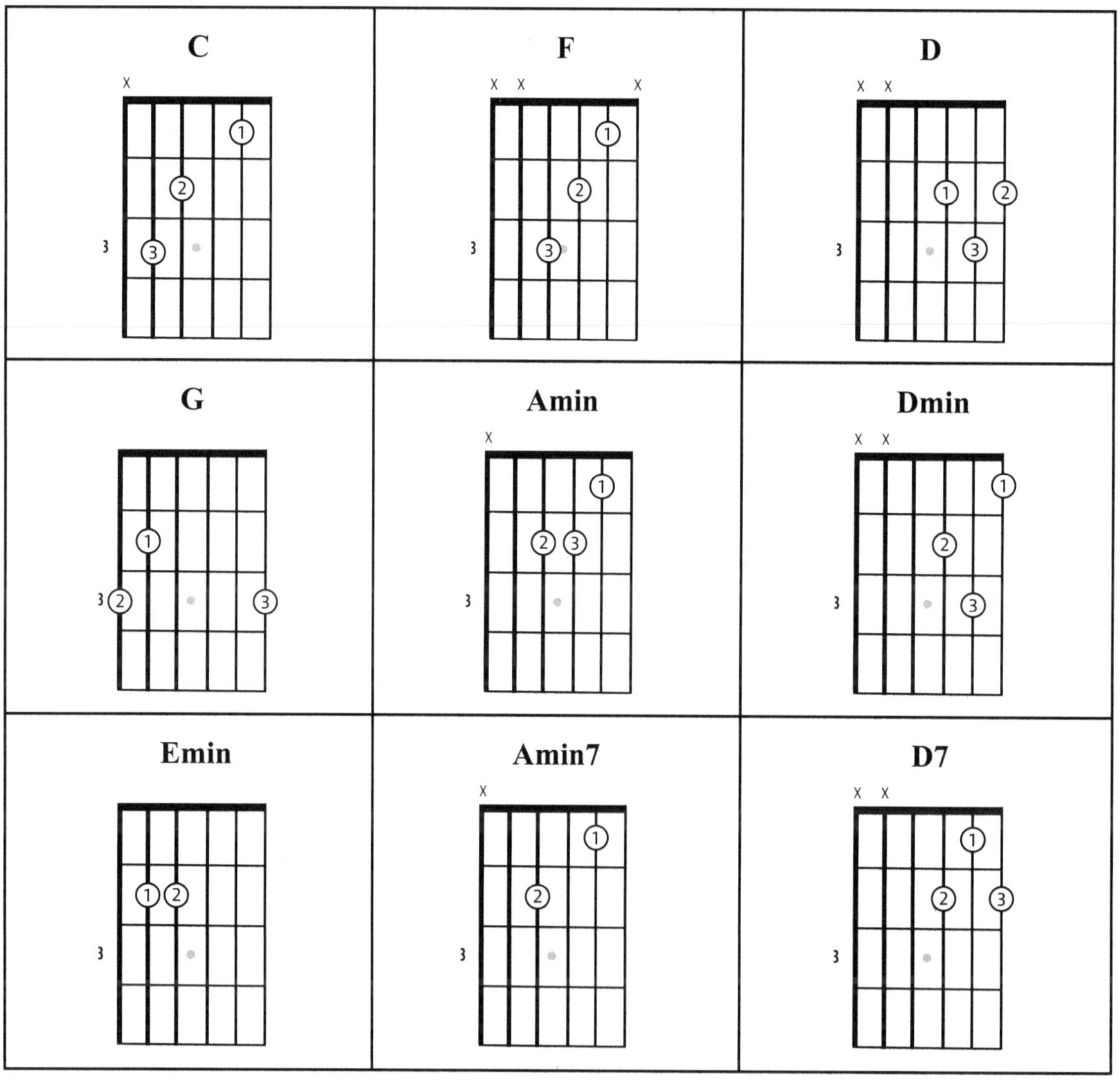

FIG. 6.1. Open Chords Group 1

Open Chords, Group 2

The open chords in group 2 are often grouped together in songs. They are: A, E, Bmin, F♯min, C♯min, E7, A7, Emin7, and B7. Start with a grouping from part 1, and practice these additional common groupings. Follow the same practice steps you used with the group 1 chords.

- People: D, Bmin, G, D; F♯min, Emin7, G, D
- New Group 1: A, C♯min, D, A, E, D
- New Group 2: E7, A7, B7, E7

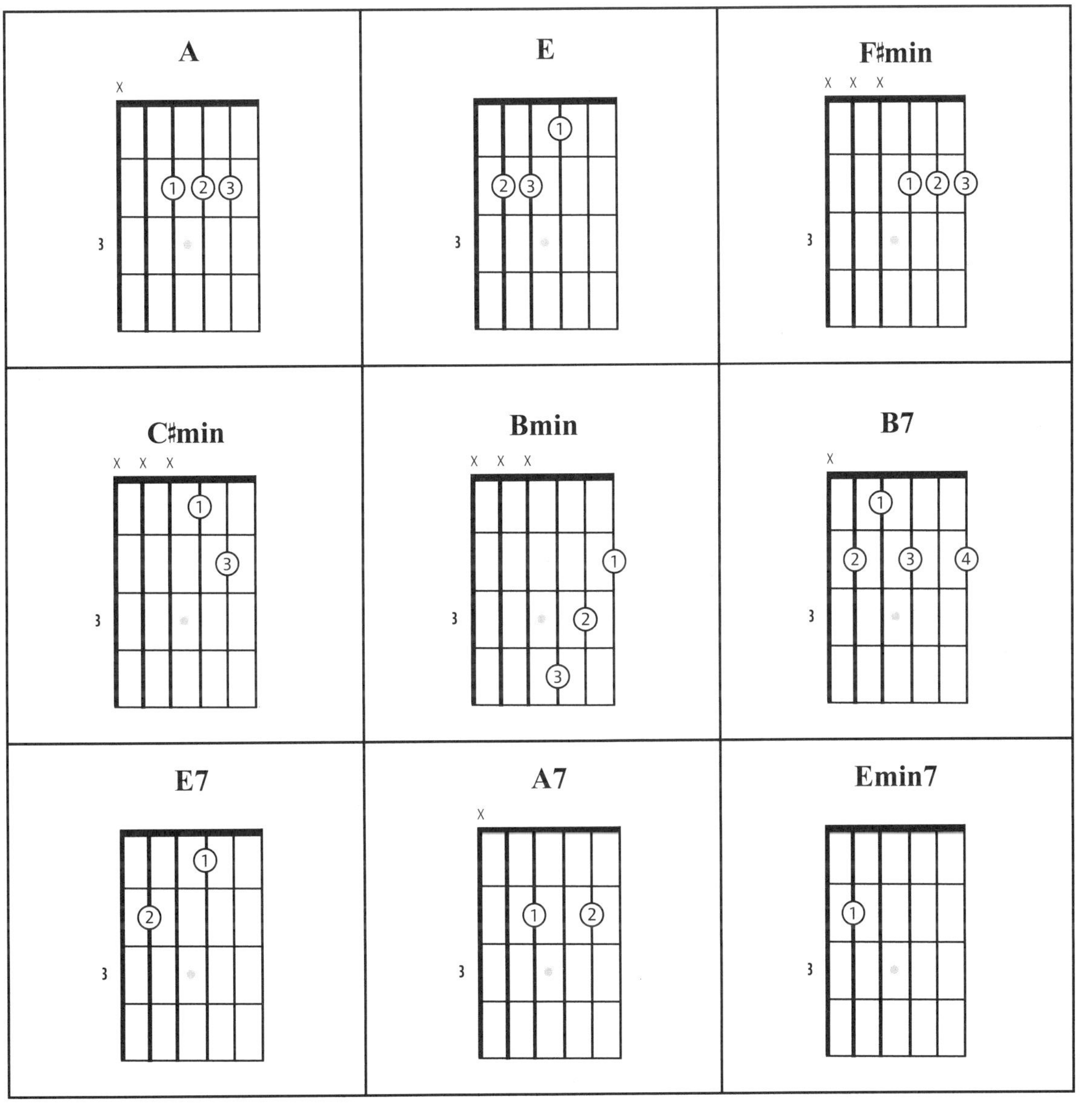

FIG. 6.2. Open Chords: Group 2

STRUMMING PATTERNS IN 4/4

Simple Split Strum

In chapter 2, you learned the simple split strum and applied it to power chord playing. This strumming pattern was originally meant for chord shapes that are played across low and high strings, and it works well with open chords. The four-beat, quarter and eighth-note rhythmic pattern is counted: 1+ 2 3+ 4. The eighth notes on beats 1 and 3 are strummed on the low strings, and the quarter notes on beats 2 and 4 on the high strings, "splitting" the chord across the strings. Accent the quarter notes to bring out the backbeat feel. The split strum is particularly effective for charts written with two chords per bar.

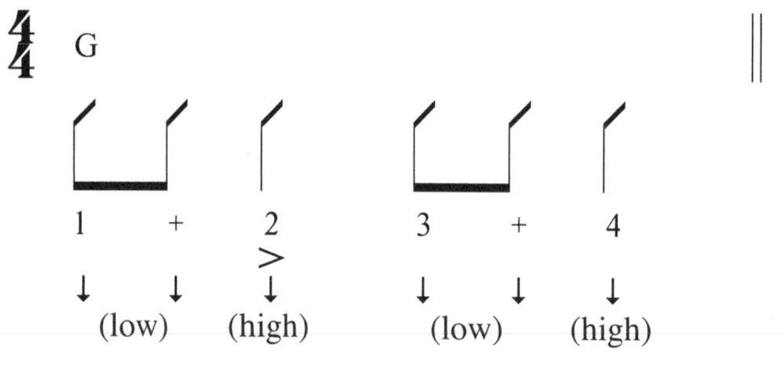

FIG. 6.3. Simple Split Strum

Complex Split Strum

The simple split strum is often developed into a more complex eighth and sixteenth-note pattern. To practice this, start by strumming beats 2 and 4 in a straight sixteenth-note rhythm—with one strum on each subdivision. As you become familiar, you may leave some of the subdivisions out and accent others, creating your own pattern on these beats.

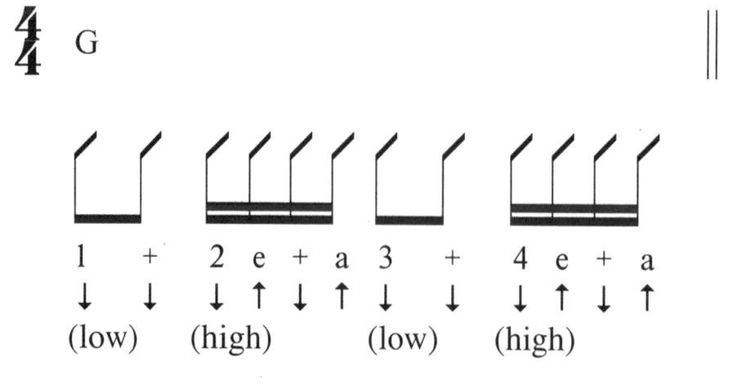

FIG. 6.4. Complex Split Strum

4/4 Folk Strum

The folk strum is a four-beat quarter-note and eighth-note pattern. You'll strum down on the beats, and up on the off beats. Take special note of the syncopation on beat 3, created by the tie in the rhythm.

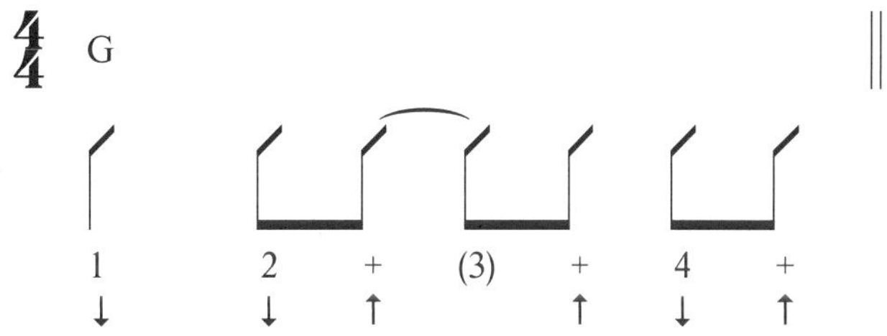

FIG. 6.5. Folk Strum

STRUMMING PATTERNS IN 3/4 AND 6/8

Triple-strum 3/4 pattern is played and written in a quarter and eighth-note rhythm, and felt "in three"—a waltz feel.

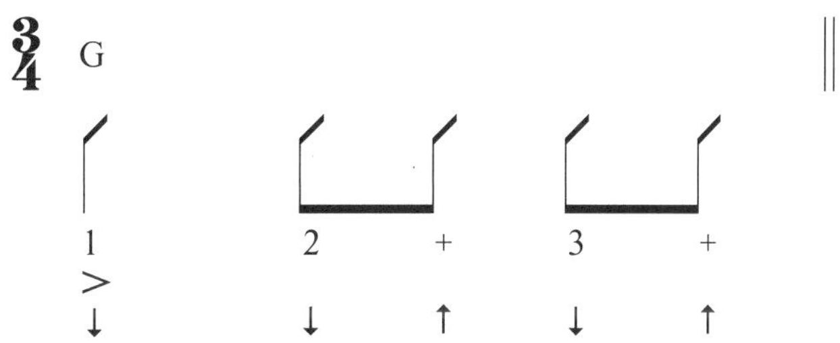

FIG. 6.6. Triple Strum 3/4

The 6/8 strum has a lilting feel, felt in two beats of three eighth notes. In music theory study, you'll learn that the pattern is counted in two beats: 1 la li, 2 la te li te, with the pulse on the numbers—a time feel called "compound time." Here, we'll use a shorthand for counting that guitar players often use for this pattern, counting each eighth note as a beat, and using "and" syllables for the subdivisions. To achieve the two-beat time feel, accent beats 1 and 4.

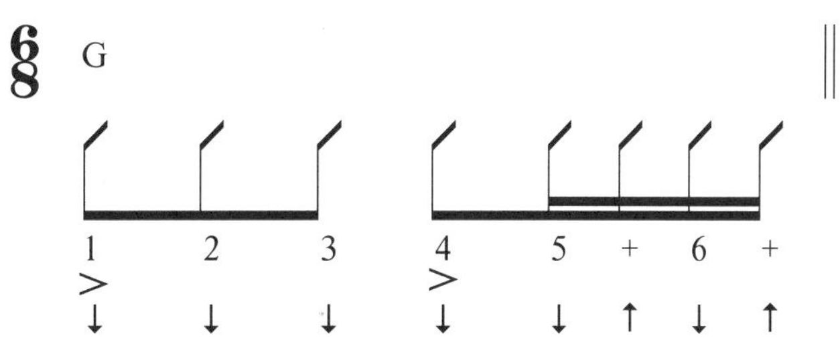

FIG. 6.7. Triple Strum 6/8

PRACTICE: STRUMMING THROUGH CHARTS

Many songs use a combination of open chords and power chords. Often in a band with two guitar players, one will play power chords in one strumming pattern, and the other will play open chords in a contrasting strumming pattern. This adds depth to the rhythm guitar parts.

Choose a chart from the examples in part IV. Practice and record yourself strumming power chords. Then, play a second part strumming open chords in the pattern of your choice. Listen for the textural contrast you are creating by layering your rhythm guitar parts. How will this approach to the rhythm guitar part affect the way you choose to play your lead guitar solo?

CHAPTER 7

Key Theory and Chord Progressions

BASIC KEY THEORY: BUILDING CHORDS

In chapter 5, we covered the theory of major scale construction. Chords are built diatonically, by stacking notes from the major scale on top of each scale degree. A "key" is the combination of the scale and the diatonic chords.

The basic diatonic chord construction is a "triad," a three-note chord built by stacking every other note of the scale from each degree. In music theory, the distance between each note in a triad is the interval of a third. Due to the pattern created by the scale, some thirds are *major* (four half steps apart in distance), and some thirds are *minor* (three half steps apart in distance). *Major* triads are built with a major third on the bottom and a minor third on top. *Minor* triads are built with a minor third on the bottom and a major third on top. This small difference in construction makes a big difference in sound!

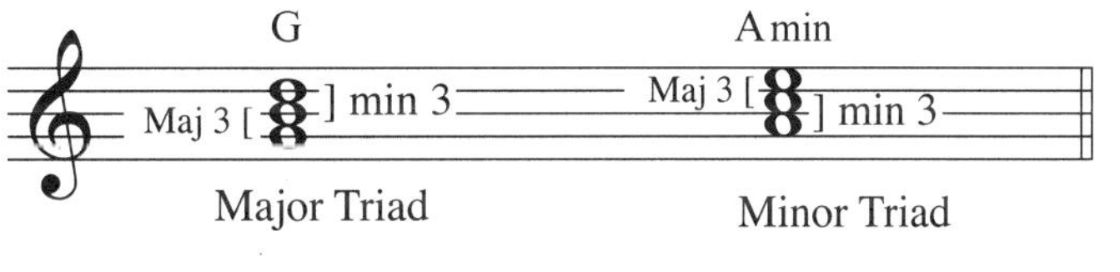

FIG. 7.1. Major and Minor Triads

The major and minor open chord shapes you learned in chapter 6 are "voicings" of triads—that is, different shapes, orders, or arrangements of the triad's notes. Some chord voicings have triad notes that are stacked diatonically (low to high), and chord voicings mix up the note order. When the order of the notes in a triad are mixed up, you are playing an "inversion" of the triad. You are still playing the same chord!

Take a look at figure 7.2, which shows an inversion of the F♯min triad (F♯, A, C♯), as fretted in our open shape.

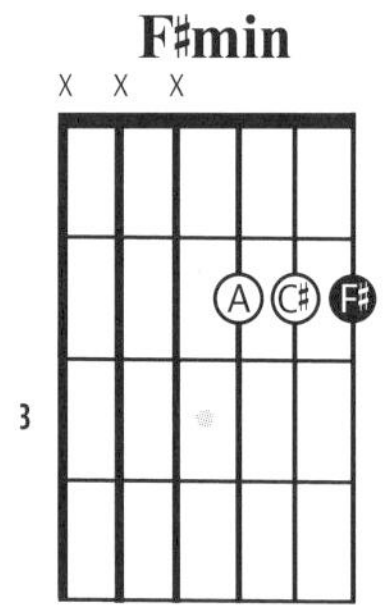

FIG. 7.2. Inversion Example, F♯min

You will play many different voicings of these triads on the fretboard, with different chord shapes. In chapter 6, you also learned "7" and "min7" chords. These are four-note diatonic chord structures called "seventh chords." We'll take a look at these and the way they fit into key theory in chapter 11.

DIATONIC TRIADS AND ROMAN NUMERALS

There is a diatonic pattern of major and minor chords in a major key. Major chords are built on scale degrees 1, 4, and 5, and minor chords are built on scale degrees 2, 3, and 6. The triad built on scale degree 7 is built with two minor thirds, and is called a "diminished triad." In this book, we'll cover major and minor triads, as they are the most common. In music theory, major chords in a key are indicated with an uppercase Roman numeral, and minor chords are indicated with uppercase Roman numeral and the suffix "min." To learn about more types of chords, refer to Rick Peckham's book (and Berklee Online class) *Berklee Guitar Chords 101.*

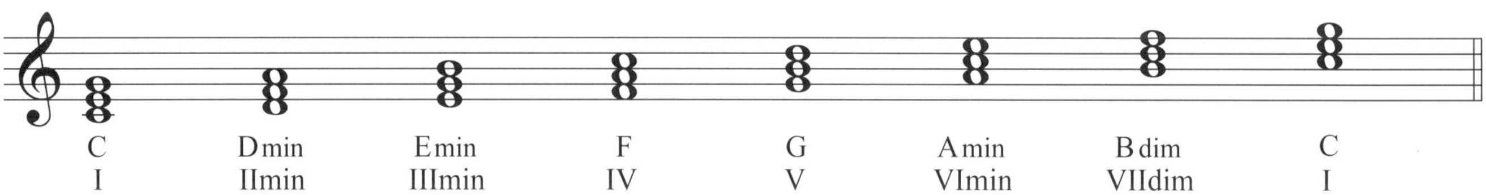

FIG. 7.3. Notation of C Major Triads with Roman Numerals

Musicians often refer to the chords by their number. For example, I may say: "This song is in C and starts on the *one* (I) chord, then goes to the *five* (V), then the *six* (VImin), and then the *four* (IV)." You would then play the chords C, G, Amin, F. Take a look at the chart for "Wisdom" in figure 7.4, with the Roman numerals indicated.

Wisdom

4/4

C	G	Amin	F	C	G	F	C
I	V	VImin	IV	I	V	IV	I

FIG. 7.4. "Wisdom," Chart with Chord Symbols and Roman Numerals

POWER CHORD CONSTRUCTION

Power chords are built diatonically with the outer notes of major and minor triads, eliminating the middle note, which determines the chord's major or minor quality. The remaining two notes are five diatonic notes apart, in the interval of a fifth. This is why power chords are written as C5 or A5: the chord symbol includes the root note and the number 5 to indicate that the second note is written a fifth above. Power chords are built on scale degrees 1, 2, 3, 4, 5, and 6 of a major scale.

FIG. 7.5. Power Chord Construction in C Major

For this reason, as you demonstrated in chapter 2, power chords can be substituted for both major and minor chords in chart playing. As a reminder, figure 7.6 shows one of those charts, written with the original chord symbols and in power chords.

Wisdom

a. Original Chords

4/4	C G	Amin F	C G	F C ‖

b. Power Chords

4/4	C5 G5	A5 F5	C5 G5	F5 C5 ‖

FIG. 7.6. "Wisdom" Chart with (a) Triads and (b) Power Chords

DETERMINING THE KEY OF A SONG CHART

One of the most common questions players ask about a new song chart is: "How do I know what key I'm in?" The answer lies with the inventory of chords in the song matched to the diatonic Roman numeral qualities of a key. For example, if you are presented with a chord chart that has the following chord progression: G D Amin C, you can determine that the song is in the key of G by matching the chords to their position in the G major scale: G = I, D = V, Amin = IImin, C = IV. To become efficient in determining keys, memorize the diatonic chords and their Roman numerals in the keys most common to popular guitar music: C, G, D, A, E. (In the key of E, you can use B7 instead of B when you are practicing this with open chords. More on why, later, in chapter 11.)

	I	IImin	IIImin	IV	V	VImin
C major	C	Dmin	Emin	F	G	Amin
G major	G	Amin	Bmin	C	D	Emin
D major	D	Emin	F♯min	G	A	Bmin
A major	A	Bmin	C♯min	D	E	F♯min
E major	E	F♯min	G♯min	A	B or B7	C♯min

If a song chart includes a melody written in standard notation, you can look at the key signature to determine the key. In chapter 5, you learned that a key signature is an inventory of the sharps and flats necessary to build the major scale from a particular root. Memorizing key signatures of common keys will help you determine the key, and what chords to expect.

Take a look at chart for "People" in figure 7.7. From the key signature and the chords included, can you see that the chart is written in the key of D major?

- C major = no sharps or flats
- G major = 1 sharp: F♯
- D major = 2 sharps: F♯, C♯
- A major = 3 sharps: F♯, C♯, G♯
- E major = 4 sharps: F♯, C♯, G♯, D♯

FIG. 7.7. "People" Chart in D Major with Key Signature

FUNCTIONAL CHORD PROGRESSIONS

Each chord in a major key has a "function"—a specific sonic role that corresponds to its numeric placement in the scale. A "chord progression"—a specific order of chords identified by their Roman numerals—has a recognizable sound regardless of key. This is why musicians think in Roman numerals to identify a key, play by ear, and "transpose"—or play the same song in different keys. To work with chord progressions, the first step is to understand the basic functions of the major and minor triads in diatonic major-key chord progressions.

Chord	Function	Description
I	Tonic	acts as home base and resolution
V	Dominant	acts as a tension chord (substitute a V7 chord for more tension)
IV	Subdominant	adds motion to the progression
IImin	(Subdominant)	a colorful substitute for IV
VImin	(Tonic)	adds additional motion to the progression
IIImin	(Tonic)	adds yet another step of motion to the progression

TRANSPOSING COMMON CHORD PROGRESSIONS

Common chord progressions in popular music order chords in strong functional patterns, and are used in many different songs. You may have already heard familiar song titles in your mind while playing the chord progressions in the example charts in this book. Change the duration of the chords in any one of the progressions, their order, or the rhythmic feel, and other songs will emerge. In this way, as you practice one song, you are also learning several similar songs. When you write your own material, you may choose to reference some of your favorite songs.

Practice the chord progressions in the following tables. Take your time working through each key, and listen to the sound of the overall chord progression.

Progression:	I	IV	V	I
Key C:	C	F	G	C
Key G:	G	C	D	G
Key D:	D	G	A	D
Key A:	A	D	E	A
Key E:	E	A	B or B7	E

Progression:	I	IImin	V	I
Key C:	C	Dmin	G	C
Key G:	G	Amin	D	G
Key D:	D	Emin	A	D
Key A:	A	Bmin	E	A
Key E:	E	F♯min	B or B7	E

Progression:	I	VImin	IV	V	I
Key C:	C	Amin	F	G	C
Key G:	G	Emin	C	D	G
Key D:	D	Bmin	G	A	D
Key A:	A	F♯min	D	E	A
Key E:	E	C♯min	A	B or B7	E

Progression:	I	VImin	IImin	V	I
Key C:	C	Amin	Dmin	G	C
Key G:	G	Emin	Amin	D	G
Key D:	D	Bmin	Emin	A	D
Key A:	A	F♯min	Bmin	E	A
Key E:	E	C♯min	F♯min	B or B7	E

Progression:	I	IIImin	IV	I
Key C:	C	Emin	F	C
Key G:	G	Bmin	C	G
Key D:	D	F♯min	G	D
Key A:	A	C♯min	D	A
Key E:	E	G♯min	A	E

CADENCES

A "cadence" is a chord progression that ends a section of a song. Knowing about them can be helpful when you're writing or learning a song by ear. Practice these common cadences in each of our five keys, and memorize the sound of each.

Name	Progression	Description
Authentic Cadence	V to I	strongest of all endings
Plagal Cadence	IV to I	softer ending, the "Amen" cadence
Deceptive Cadence	V to VImin	surprises the listener; look for it in a song at the bridge
Authentic Half Cadence	? to V	unfinished, leaves you hanging
Plagal Half Cadence	End on IV	common in folk music, not as dramatic as an authentic half cadence, leaves an open ending

PRACTICE: ANALYZE AND TRANSPOSE CHARTS

Turn to part IV, and analyze the practice charts. Before the notation, you'll find the key of each chart. Write in the Roman numerals for each chord symbol. Now, transpose each chart into our common keys, using the tables here in chapter 7 to check your work. As you work on your rhythm and lead guitar parts in each key, listen to the sonic differences of each. This is an effective way to practice many chord shapes and scale patterns, and deep way to get to know each key center.

CHAPTER 8

Fingerstyle Techniques

Fingerstyle picking patterns are standard to guitar playing, and often used in rhythm guitar parts. Classical players, in particular, have developed a technique that allows for maximum tone production, facility, and hand health. The basic approach we'll cover here will set you up for both classical and fingerstyle playing. For an in-depth approach to these techniques, refer to my book *Classical Technique for the Modern Guitarist* (Kim Perlak, Berklee Press 2016).

PICKING-HAND POSITION

You'll remember from chapter 1 that the basic picking-hand position can be found by draping your right arm diagonally across the guitar body. For fingerpicking and classical style picking-hand technique, your arm will meet the guitar body mid-forearm or near your elbow depending on the body size of your instrument. Just as when you play using a pick, your fingers will cross the strings diagonally (see figure 1.7).

Arm Rests on Guitar Body

Thumbnail on String

FIG. 8.1. Picking Hand Position

You'll also remember the three important aspects of wrist alignment in your picking-hand position: *angle, height,* and *tilt* (see figure 1.5). As a review: with angle, aim for a straight wrist, aligning your hand with your arm. For height, make sure the big knuckles of your hand are higher or at the same height as your wrist joint. With tilt, rotate your hand and forearm as if you are turning a doorknob. Tilt your hand toward the pinky-side to support your weaker fingers. Together, these elements of alignment result in healthy technique and a full sound. Remember: The picking-hand fingers are labeled: thumb = *p*, index = *i*, middle = *m*, ring = *a*, pinky = *c*.

Set up your picking hand with the fingers *p, i, m,* and *a* on strings ④, ③, ②, and ①. Find your angle, height, and tilt. Let your *c* finger curve into your palm, moving with *m* and *a*. Practice finding your position by taking your hand off the strings and putting it on again.

"PICKING" WITH YOUR THUMB

Once you are comfortable with a basic picking-hand position, you're ready to play with your thumb. With the edge of your thumb (*p*), press into string ④. Find the spot on the pad of your thumb that feels secure while still allowing you to play the string. This is your *contact point*. The amount of weight you place on your contact point at this moment will determine your volume. Next, play the string on a downward angle. Your thumb should clear the other strings and land, as dead weight, on to your index finger (*i*) at the tip-joint knuckle. Work with your parameters of sound from chapter 5 as you are playing: dynamics, timbre, and envelope. Practice these steps on open strings ⑤ and ⑥, and then with your favorite patterns of the pentatonic scale on the same strings.

Next, apply this technique in your reading of melodies on the bass strings. When warming up, improvising, and reading, play with awareness of technique and tone—and remember to breathe!

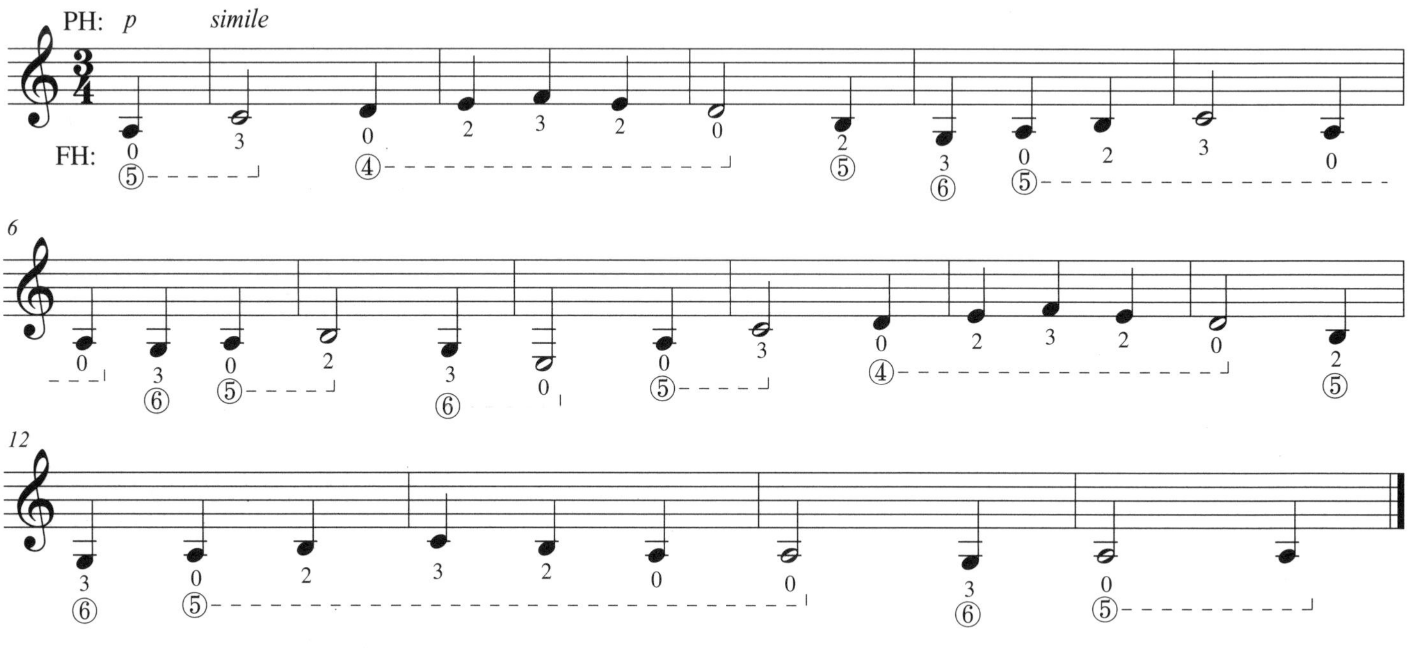

FIG. 8.2. Thumb Melody. PH = Picking Hand, FH = Fretting Hand.

BASIC FINGER MOTIONS

Find your hand position once again on strings ④, ③, ②, and ①. Leave your thumb on string ④ for balance, and press into strings ③, ②, and ① with fingers *i*, *m*, and *a* to find your contact point on each. With your thumb resting on string ④, play fingers *i*, *m*, and *a* together back into your hand from the big knuckle joint—as though you're making a loose fist. As you play, pay attention to your hand position and your tone.

Next, practice playing each finger individually. Keep your thumb resting on string ④, and place only the finger you are playing on a treble string. Practice *i* on ③, *m* on ②, and *a* on ①. The fingers that are not playing should loosely follow through into your hand as you play. As always, maintain awareness of tone and technique, and breathe!

Melodic Alternation: *i* and *m*

Alternating fingers *i* and *m* is the standard technique for playing scales and melodies. To practice alternation, rest your thumb on string ④. Place your *i* finger on string ③, keeping the remaining three fingers loosely curved in your hand. Push into the string with *i*, noting that the amount of weight will determine your dynamic level. Play your *i* finger back into your hand from the big knuckle joint. As you play *i*, gently kick out your *m* finger, allowing your *a* and *c* fingers to move with *m*. This "scissor" motion readies your *m* finger just above the string. Now, place *m* on string ③, and push in with the same amount of weight. As you play *m*, allow *a* and *c* to gently follow through as well, and kick out with *i*.

Next, practice crossing strings with alternation. Resting your thumb on string ④, move your fingers diagonally towards the bridge to practice alternation on string ②, and then on string ①. Notice that this motion is similar to your strumming motion! By crossing the strings on a diagonal, you'll maintain the same hand position while playing each string. Consistent position creates consistent tone.

Practice crossing strings with alternation using figure 8.3. Break up the melody into small sections to work on this technique, and focus on your tone as you play.

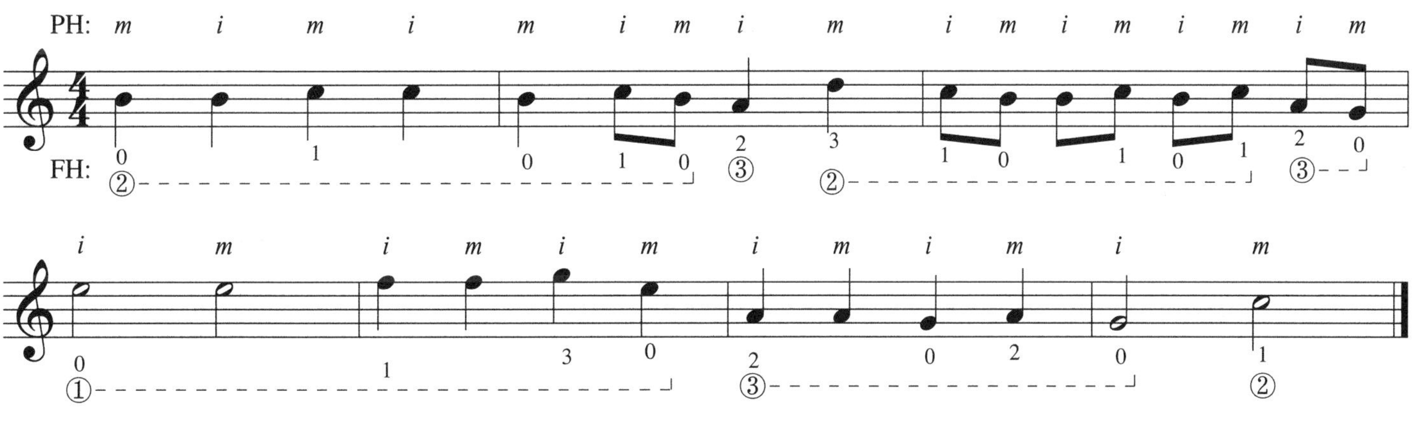

FIG. 8.3. Finger Alternation Melody. PH = Picking Hand, FH = Fretting Hand.

FINGERPICKING PATTERNS

There are three fingerpicking patterns common to classical playing and to popular and traditional styles. In a band context, these fingerpicking patterns can be used as rhythm guitar parts. Practice each pattern on open strings, focusing on hand position, technique, and tone. Then, work on the material in the examples.

Thumb and Finger Alternation

The thumb and finger alternation is an eighth-note pattern, with *p* playing a bass note on the beat and a finger (or fingers) playing the off-beats. Begin by placing *p* on string ⑤, *i* on string ③, and *m* on string ②. Play *p*, letting it follow through. Play *i* and *m* together, back into your palm. At the same time, return your thumb to string ⑤. As you play *p* again, return *i* and *m* to strings ③ and ②. Repeat this alternation. Next, repeat these steps, alternating: *p* and *i*, and *p* and *m*.

Pick through the example in figure 8.4, using each finger and string combination. As you play through charts with this pattern, you may make your own creative choices!

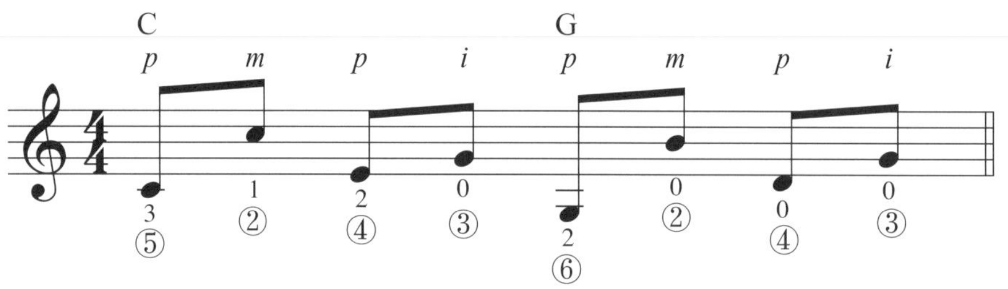

FIG. 8.4. Thumb and Finger Alternation Pattern

Travis Pick

Named after the Nashville guitarist Merle Travis, the *Travis pick* is a four-beat, eighth-note pattern. In this pattern, you'll assign pairs of fingers to an "outside" and an "inside" pair of strings, depending on which open chord you're fretting. Assign *p* and *m* to the outside string pair, ⑤ and ②. Assign *p* and *i* to the inside string pair, ④ and ③. Take a look the Travis pick fingering and rhythm, shown in figure 8.5. Practice the pattern open strings, and then fret the C chord. As practice with other chords, you'll choose the string pairs!

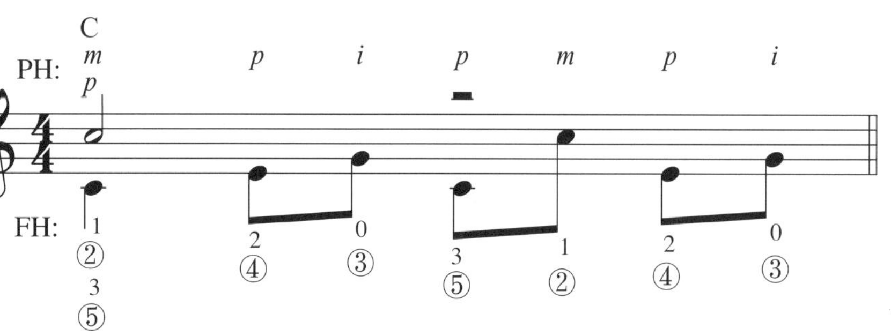

FIG. 8.5. Travis Pick Pattern

Thumb and Two Fingers

The thumb-and-two-fingers pattern is used to play notes grouped in three. The standard pattern is played on three strings, with the fingers *p, i, m*. Assign *p, i, m* to three strings, for example ⑤, ③, ②. Place *p* on string ⑤. As you play *p*, set up *i* and *m* on strings ③ and ②. Play *i* individually. As you play *m* individually, reset *p* on ⑤. Play the pattern as written in figure 8.6. When you play a chart, you'll choose the string set for each chord.

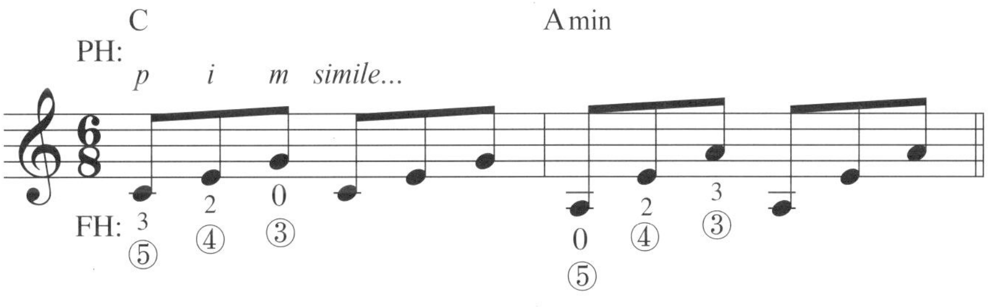

FIG. 8.6. Thumb-and-Two-Fingers (Triple-Time) Pattern

PRACTICE: PICKING THROUGH CHARTS

In chart playing, fingerpicking patterns can be used in the place of strumming patterns. At times, the patterns will be written into the chart in notation, and other times their use will be left up to the discretion of the player. Take a look at the chart for "Prayer" in part IV, and learn the written fingerpicking pattern. Next, take a look at one of the other charts suggests that fingerpicking may be used as a rhythm part. Which patterns would fit best, given the structure of the chart? Use the lessons in this chapter for reference, and experiment!

PART II REVIEW

At this point, you have built on your basic guitar foundation of basic guitar and have developed a broad set of skills that will allow you to hear, understand, play, and write popular songs in a variety of styles. Take a moment to breathe and reflect on how far you have come in your playing!

Next, go back to each chapter and make a plan to review and rotate each of these materials each day that you practice: pentatonic scale theory, five patterns of the pentatonic scale, open chords, strumming patterns, key theory, common chord progressions, and fingerpicking patterns. Have some fun recording rhythm guitar tracks and improvising guitar solos with your favorite songs. When you have an opportunity, try playing songs with others. Revisit materials from part 1: notate your chord charts and melodies, and continue to work on your tone with the parameters of sound.

Enjoy your practice and all its possibilities!

Part III

Beyond "Beginner"

These next four chapters introduce materials, concepts, and playing strategies that will take your guitar playing to the next level and open more creative doors. In chapter 9, we'll explore the modes, scales that will bring color to your playing and ground you in a variety of styles. Chapter 10 introduces a set of moveable triad shapes that will allow you to explore higher registers of the fretboard with familiar chords. Chapter 11 delves deeper into chord theory and applications that bring a sense of motion, tension, and arrival to your playing. Chapter 12 introduces the twelve-bar blues, a true American roots style that has influenced every style of contemporary popular music.

These materials will continue to strengthen your foundation and open your ears more and more to what possibilities may lie ahead in your guitar journey.

CHAPTER 9

Modes of the Major Scale

Modes are created by starting a scale on each note. Because there are seven notes in the major scale, there are seven modes with seven fingering patterns on the fretboard. Each mode has a distinctive sound that is useful for songwriting. Later in your study, you may also use the modes to improvise with complex chord changes in jazz and other styles. Rick Peckham's book *Modal Voicings for Guitar* (Berklee Press, 2020) is a great resource on this topic.

SCALE THEORY: MAJOR MODES

Remember the music theory of major scale construction we covered in chapter 5? The theory of major modes begins with the major scale. When you treat each different scale degree of the major scale as the tonic, or musical home base, you are playing in modes of the scale. Each mode starts on a different scale degree and has a different name. Because the modes of a major scale contain the same notes, the first mode is called the "parent key." The following table shows the modes in the parent key of C major: the starting scale degrees, modal names, and the notes within each.

MODES OF C MAJOR

Starting Scale Degree	Mode Name	Notes of C Major Modes
1	Ionian	C D E F G A B C
2	Dorian	D E F G A B C D
3	Phrygian	E F G A B C D E
4	Lydian	F G A B C D E F
5	Mixolydian	G A B C D E F G
6	Aeolian	A B C D E F G A
7	Locrian	B C D E F G A B

Mode Naming

There are two ways to name the modes, depending on their intended use. If you want to stay in the sound of the parent scale and play in the different modal patterns, you would say you are playing "C major from the 5th degree," or "C major from the 6th degree." You are playing the C major scale, the Ionian mode, up and down the fretboard. From this perspective, each mode is "relative" to the parent scale.

If you want to bring out the changes in the sound color and character of each different mode, you will treat each new starting scale degree as a tonic. The change in the position of the half steps within the scale as you tonicize each different degree changes the mood of the scale. In this case, you are looking at the modes from a "parallel" perspective to one another by tone color, and you would call the mode you've chosen by its mode name: Mixolydian, Dorian, or Aeolian.

Remember your work with the pentatonics in chapters 2 and 5? You have already explored these modal perspectives!

For a comprehensive approach to the modes on the guitar, please see *Berklee Guitar Theory* (curated by Kim Perlak, Berklee Press 2023).

MODAL FINGERING PATTERNS

There are seven notes in the major scale, and seven moveable fingering patterns that begin on each scale degree. In the figure 9.1 fingering diagrams, each of the modal patterns are shown in the parent key of C major. You can be play them in any key by setting them up on the fretboard on your intended root note.

C Major from First Degree	C Major
Parent Scale Degrees	Mode Degrees (Identical to Parent Scale)
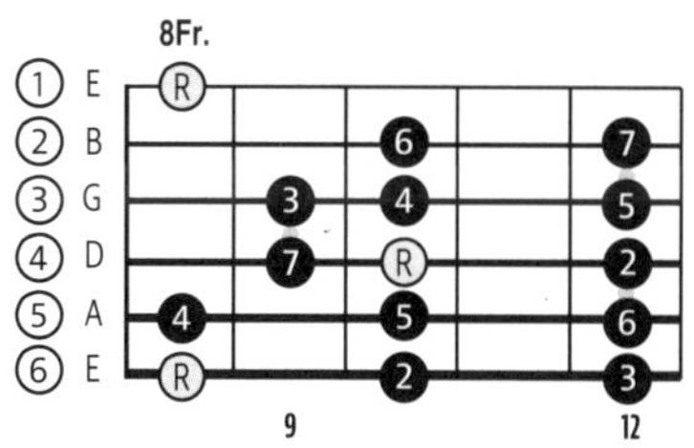	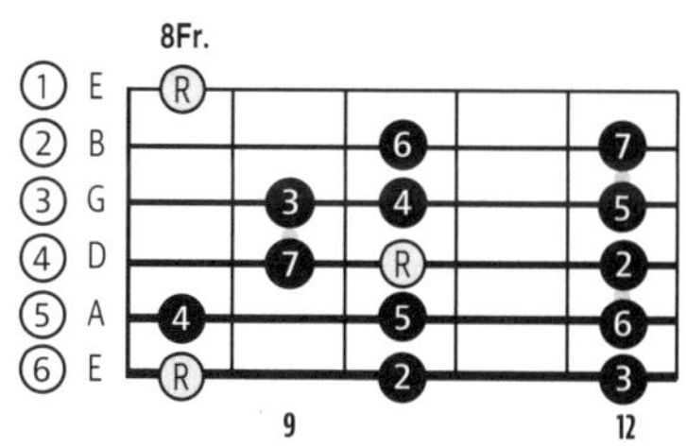

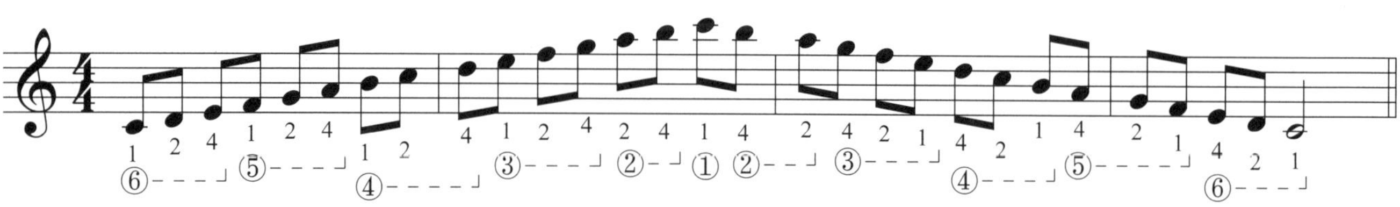

C Major from Second Degree	D Dorian
Parent Scale Degrees	Mode Degrees
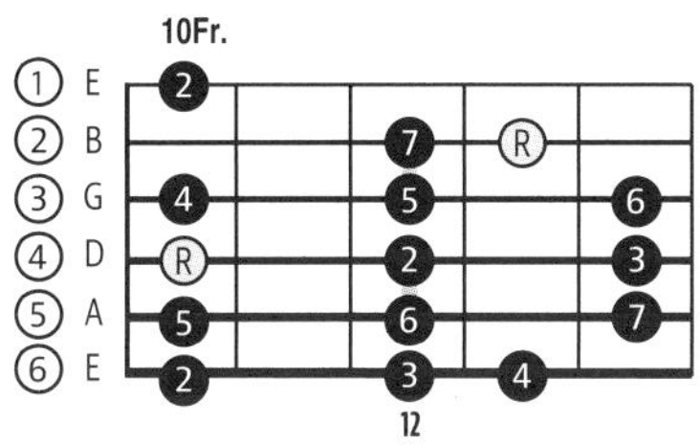	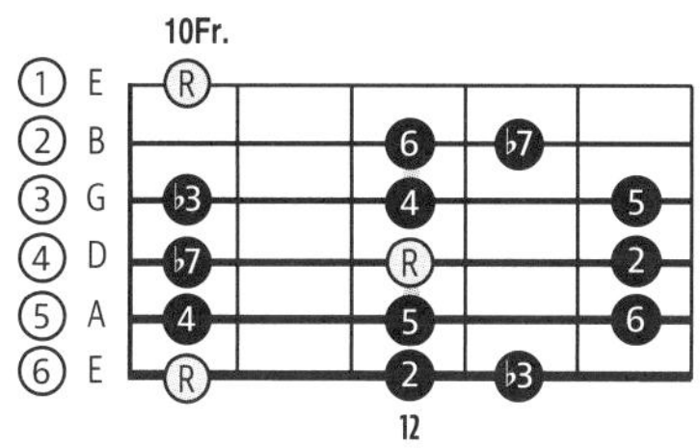

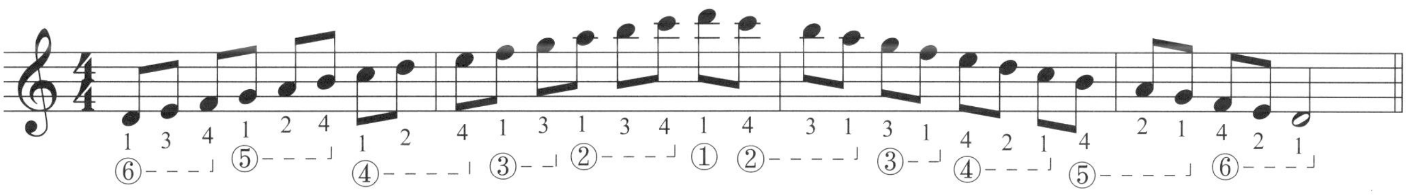

C Major from Third Degree	E Phrygian
Parent Scale Degrees	Mode Degrees
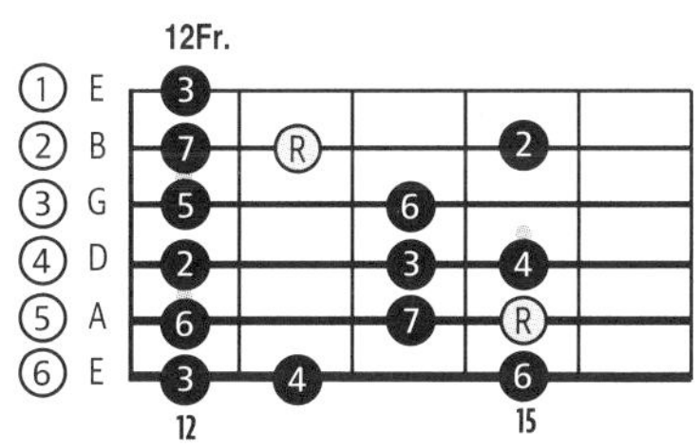	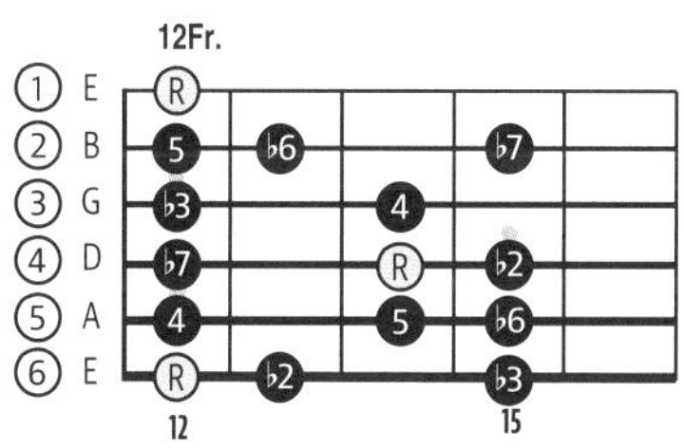

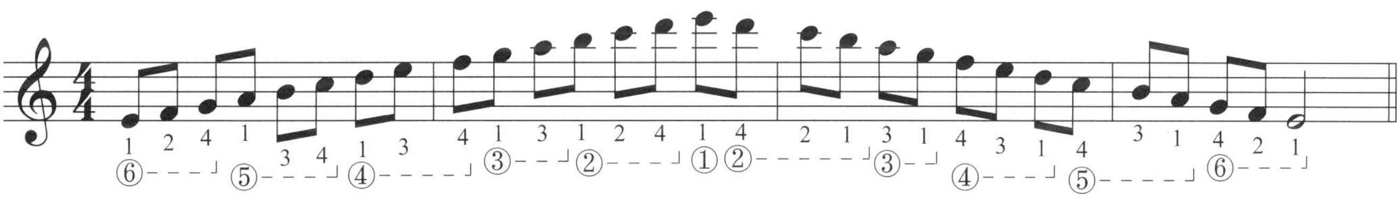

C Major from Fourth Degree	F Lydian
Parent Scale Degrees	Mode Degrees
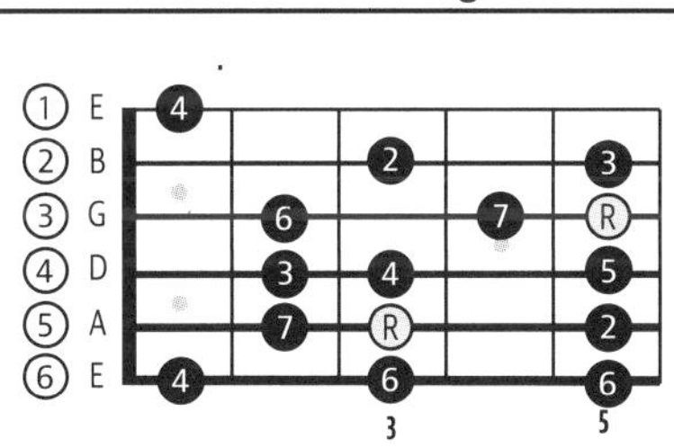	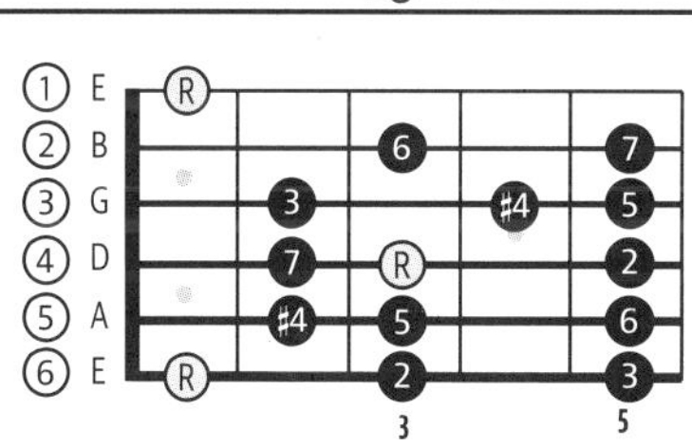

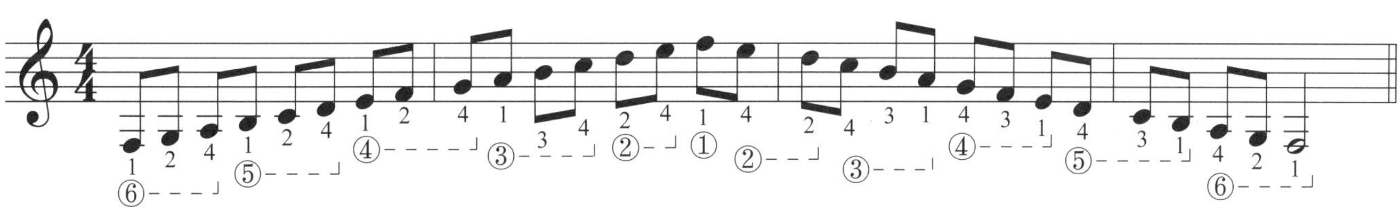

C Major from Fifth Degree	G Mixolydian
Parent Scale Degrees	Mode Degrees

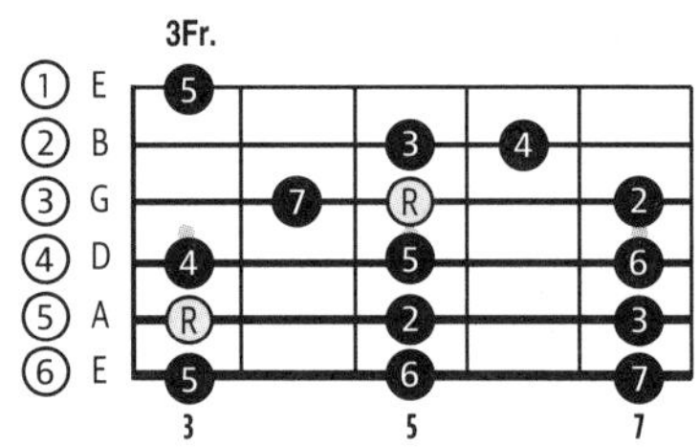

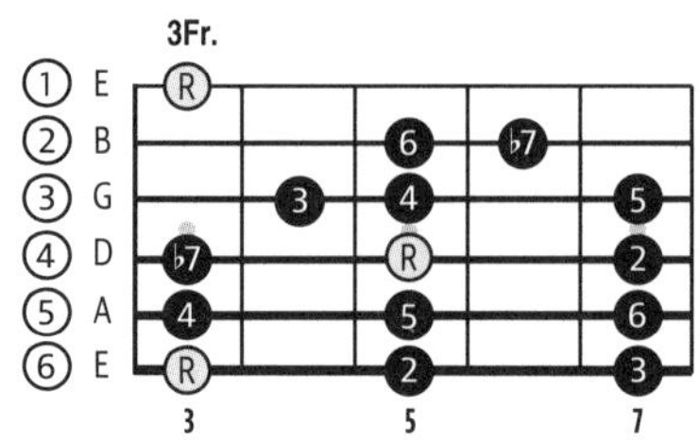

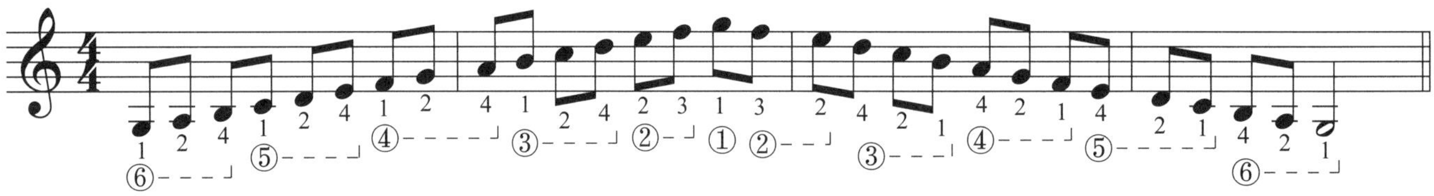

C Major from Sixth Degree	A Aeolian
Parent Scale Degrees	Mode Degrees

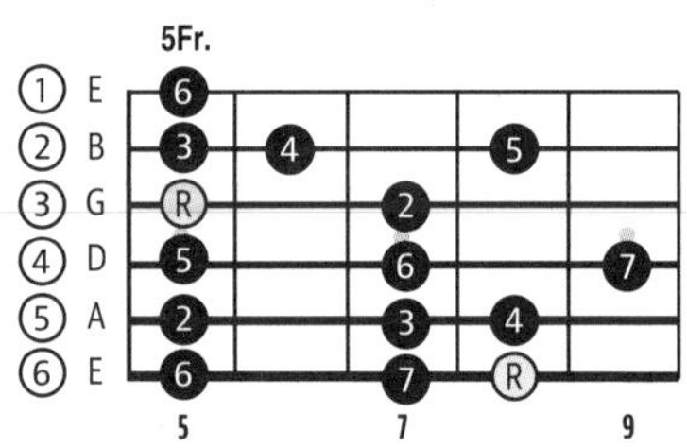

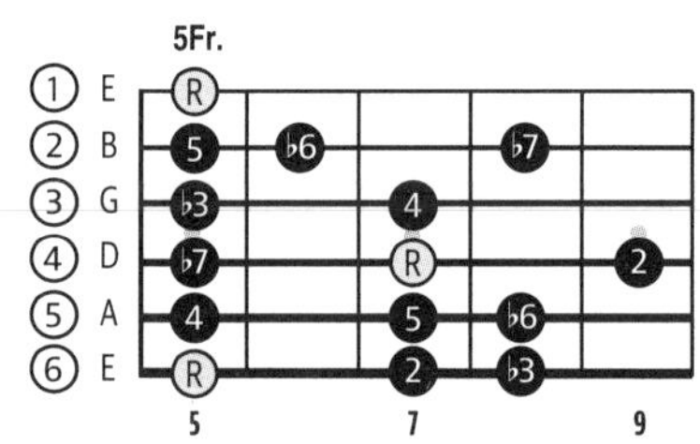

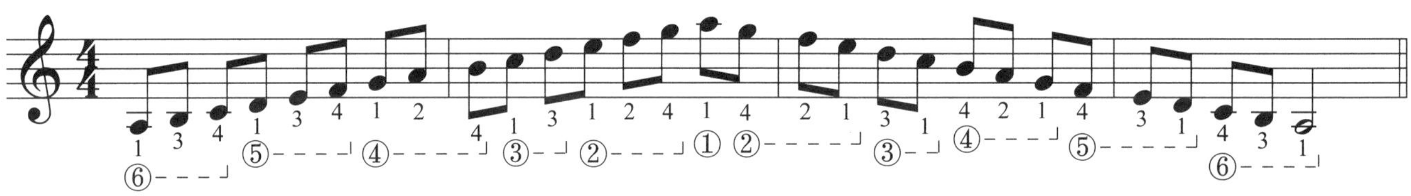

C Major from Seventh Degree	B Locrian
Parent Scale Degrees	Mode Degrees

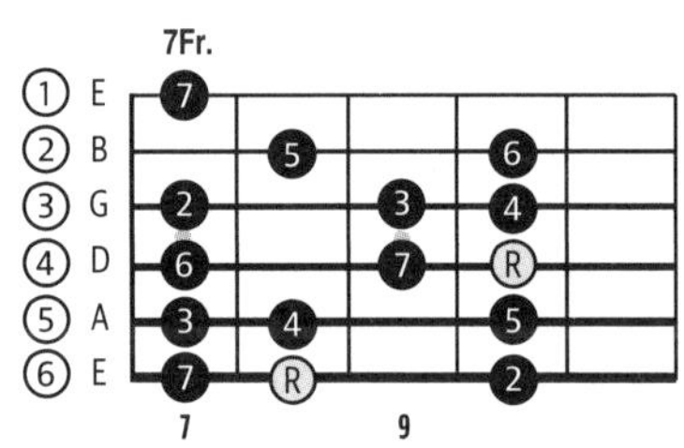

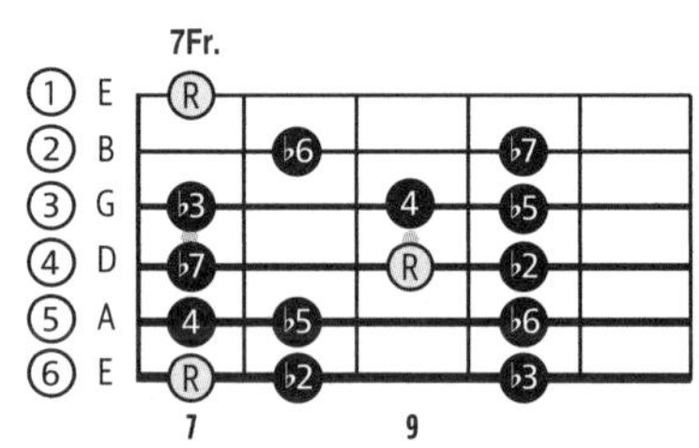

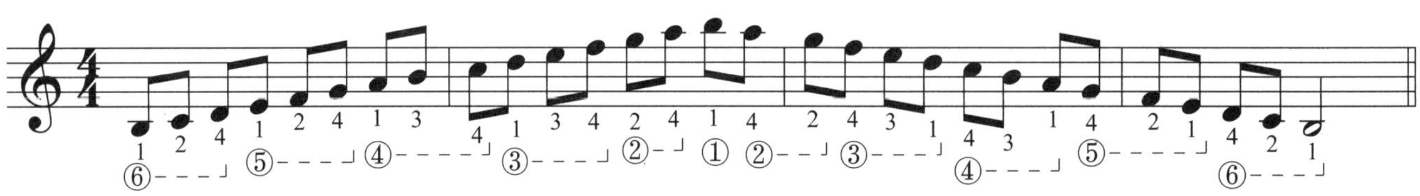

FIG. 9.1. Modes of the C Major Scale

IMPROVISING WITH MODAL COLORS

When you tonicize the start-note of each mode, you pull your listeners' ears to the chord built on that scale degree. These combined materials create the mood, or color, of each mode. Modal colors add drama and interest to songwriting, composition, and improvisation. The following table lists the modes of C major by their start note, the chord that becomes the modal tonic, their distinctive color.

Mode	Chord	Color
C Ionian	C (I)	major sound
D Dorian	Dmin (IImin)	brighter than minor
E Phrygian	Emin (IIImin)	darker than minor
F Lydian	F (IV)	brighter than major
G Mixolydian	G (V)	darker than major
A Aeolian	Amin (VImin)	natural minor sound
B Locrian	B° (VII°)	colorful and unlike major or minor

PRACTICE: MODAL IMPROVISATION

To build your familiarity with the modal colors, improvise with a one-chord vamp (repeated rhythm) on the tonic chord of each major mode.

1. Create a one-chord vamp for the Ionian mode, by recording yourself strumming the C chord in time for at least one minute.
2. Improvise melodies with the Ionian mode fingering, mode 1. Let the sound of the mode wash over you as you improvise.

Repeat this process for the next five modes: Dorian (IImin), Phrygian (IIImin), Lydian (IV), Mixolydian (V), Aeolian (VImin). The Locrian mode is centered on the B diminished triad (VII°). Because of its unstable nature, this triad and its related mode are not often used in popular music. For this reason, the exercises in this book cover the first six triads in major keys, and six modes of the major scale.

The more you improvise with these modal vamps, the more distinct the color of each mode will become, and you'll start to recognize these colors in songs you know.

C Ionian Vamp

4/4 ||: C | C | C | C :||

D Dorian Vamp

4/4 ||: Dmin | Dmin | Dmin | Dmin :||

E Phrygian Vamp

4/4 ||: Emin | Emin | Emin | Emin :||

F Lydian Vamp

4/4 ||: F | F | F | F :||

G Mixolydian Vamp

4/4 ||: G | G | G | G :||

A Aeolian Vamp

4/4 ||: Amin | Amin | Amin | Amin :||

FIG. 9.2. One-Chord Modal Vamps

Now that you've played through the modal vamp exercise, take it one step deeper: Remember that each mode of the major scale is built with the same notes! This means that you can improvise with any of the seven patterns and create the modal color of your choice. You'll do this by treating the start note of your chosen mode as your tonic, no matter which fingering pattern you choose. This is how players improvise up and down the entire fretboard, creating the sound colors of their choice. Try this approach with your modal vamps, and listen to the colors you create!

PHRASING TECHNIQUES: SLURS

Now you've learned the fingering patterns of the major modes, three slur techniques will add interest to your phrasing in improvisation. *Hammer-ons*, *pull-offs*, and *slides* connect consecutive notes in a scale pattern with nuance. All three techniques are called "slurs" because of the way they connect two notes without leaving space between them.

To practice slurs, fret your modal pattern Aeolian/C major from the 6th degree, and go to string ④. Use two notes on that string in the pattern, on the 5th and 7th frets.

To *hammer-on*, fret the note on string ④ 5th fret with your first finger, and play it. While the note is still ringing and your first finger is still pressing down, use your third finger as a hammer to strike the 7th fret. Keep your third finger pressed on the 7th fret to sustain the second note.

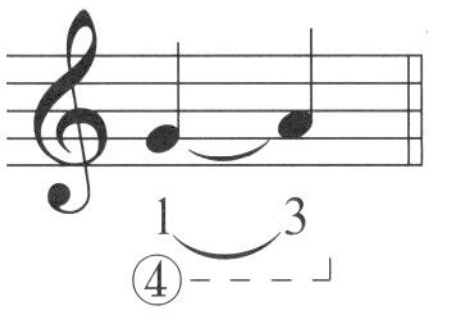

FIG. 9.3. Hammer-On

To *pull-off,* fret both notes on string ④: the 5th fret with your first finger and 7th fret with your third finger. Play string ④, and then pull your third finger off the string, plucking the second note with your third finger.

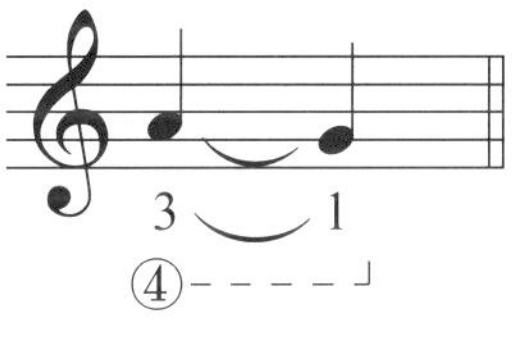

FIG. 9.4. Pull-Off

To *slide* between these same two notes, fret the 5th fret note with your third finger. Play that note, and while it is still ringing, slide your third finger up to the 7th fret. Keep the pressure down as you slide, and you'll hear both notes!

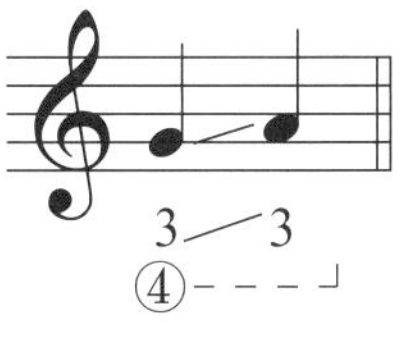

FIG. 9.5. Slide

PRACTICE: SLUR EXERCISES

Practice your slurs on the fretboard with two exercises: "Slur Walking," and "Slurs with Modal Patterns." "Slur walking" is similar to the "fretting-hand walking" warm-up you practiced in chapter 1: you'll "walk" each slur across the strings in one position on the fretboard.

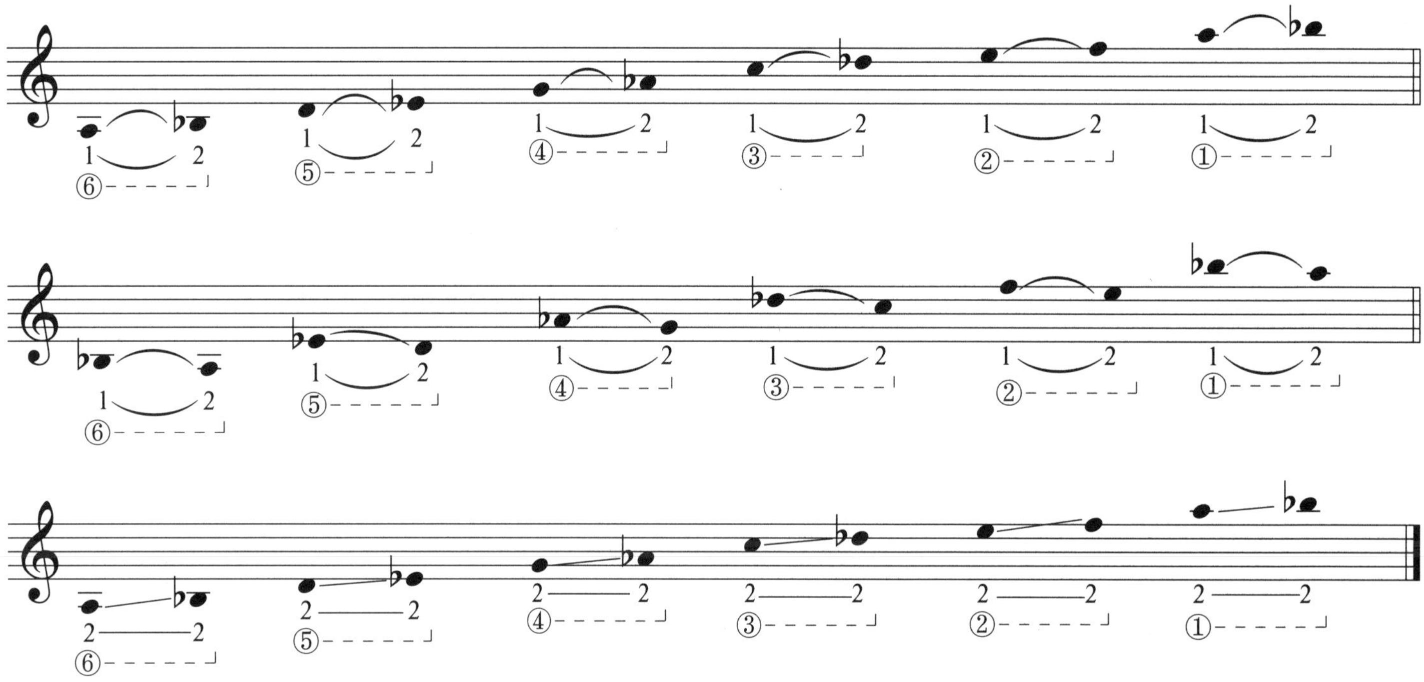

FIG. 9.6. Slur Walking

In this modal pattern exercise, you'll practice your slurs using a scale fingering.

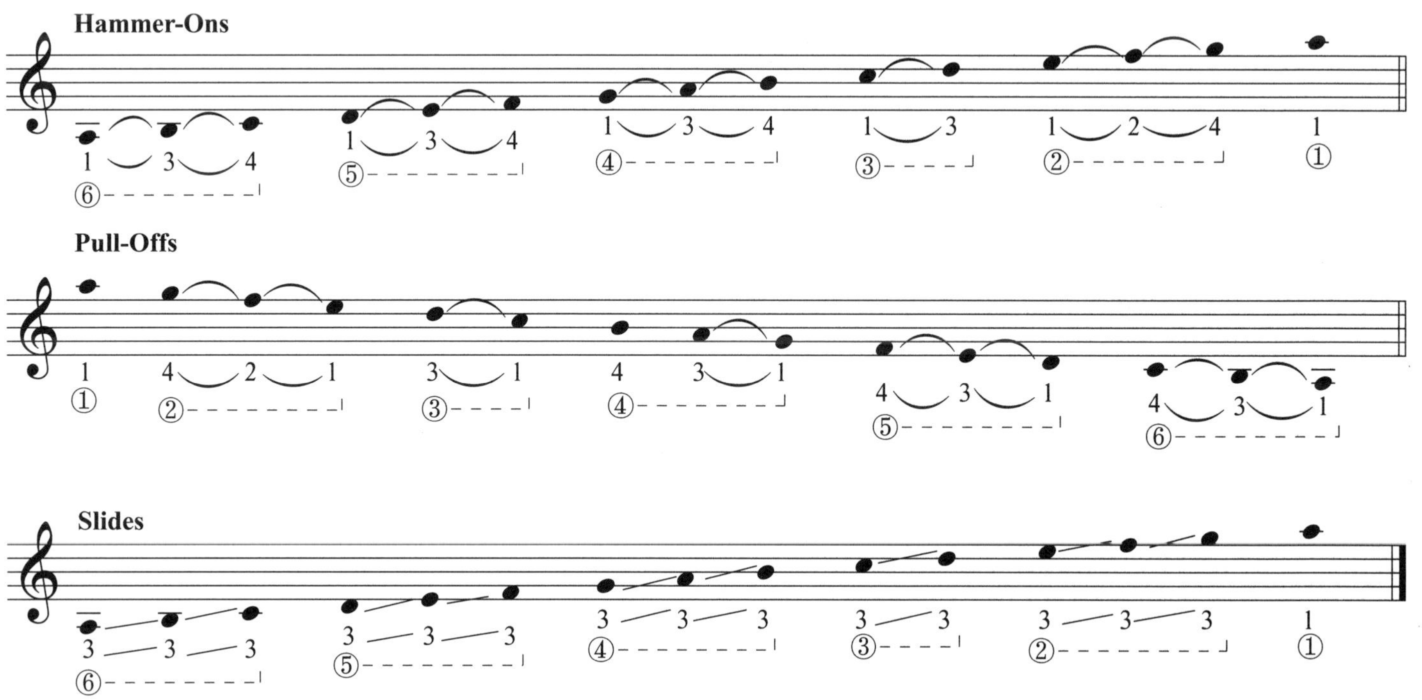

FIG. 9.7. Slurs with Modal Patterns

PRACTICE: WRITING AND PLAYING RIFFS AND PHRASES

In many popular songs, hammer-ons, pull-offs, and slides are often used in riffs and melodic phrases. To experiment with these techniques, improvise in a modal pattern with one of the vamps from the exercises, and incorporate slurs to bring out the nuances of your phrasing. Record your improvisations, and notate your favorite riffs and phrases. Keep a collection of them, and use them as you craft longer solos. Listen for the big difference small changes make as you play them: the difference in sound between a slide, hammer-on, pull-off—a change in rhythm, dynamics, timbre. Use slurs in your pentatonic practice as well.

CHAPTER 10

Moveable Triad Shapes

Moveable triad shapes allow you to play a large number of triad chords on different parts of the fretboard. These shapes are found on all sets of three adjacent strings on the guitar. In this chapter, we'll cover major and minor triad shapes on string set ③②①. With moveable triad shapes, you can voice chords in a complementary register to open chords and power chords.

MAJOR TRIAD SHAPES ON STRING SET ③②①

Remember from chapter 7 that a major triad is a chord built with three notes, in intervals of a major and minor third. The chord tones of a major triad correspond to the first, third, and fifth scale degrees of the major scale: 1, 3, 5. The three major triad voicings on string set ③②① are:

		Major Scale Degrees on Strings		
		③	②	①
Inversion	Root Position	1	3	5
	First Inversion	3	5	1
	Second Inversion	5	1	3

To fret major triads with these shapes, you'll use the names of the notes on strings ③, ②, and ①. Match the root of the major triad you want to play with the shape you choose. You'll strum only the strings you are fretting. For fingerings, use the option that fits your hand the best, favoring the strongest fingers (1, 2, 3) when possible.

Here, in figure 10.1, are the three major triad voicings, fretted as C major chords:

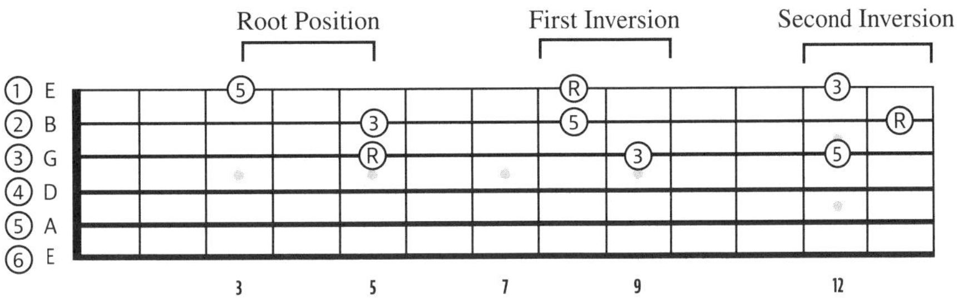

FIG. 10.1. C Major Triads: Root Position, First Inversion, Second Inversion

MINOR TRIAD SHAPES ON STRING SET ③②①

Minor triads are built with stacked intervals of a minor third and a major third. The chord tones of a minor triad correspond to the first, flat-third, and fifth scale degrees of the major scale: 1, ♭3, 5. The three minor triad shapes and their voicings on string set ③②① are:

Inversion	Minor Scale Degrees on Strings ③	②	①
Root Position	1	♭3	5
First Inversion	♭3	5	1
Second Inversion	5	1	♭3

To fret minor chords using these shapes, you'll use the note names of the notes on strings ③②①. Match the root note of the minor chord you want to play with the shape you choose. Once you've memorized your major triad shapes, lower the third by one fret and adjust your fingering to fret the minor shapes. Strum only the strings you are fretting. Here, in figure 10.2, are the three minor triad voicings fretted as C minor chord shapes.

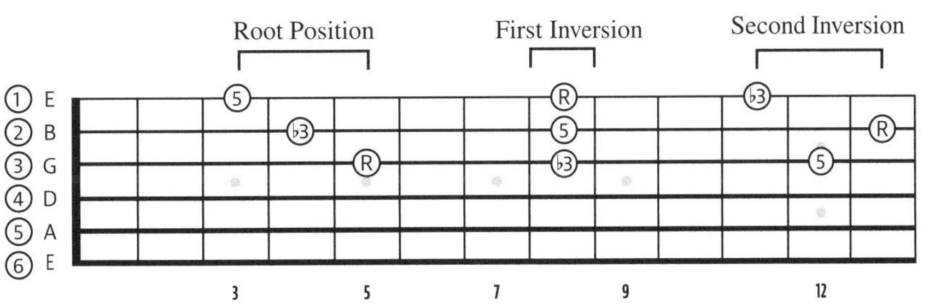

FIG. 10.2. C Minor Triads: Root Position, First Inversion, Second Inversion

PLAYING CHORD PROGRESSIONS WITH MOVEABLE TRIADS

Remember the common chord progressions from chapter 7? Now, play them using moveable major and minor triad shapes. Because there are three shapes for each triad, there are multiple ways to play each progression. Start with the following pathway, applying the shapes to each key. Go slowly, learning each progression in one key at a time.

Progression:	I	IV	V	I
	First Inversion	Root Position	Second Inversion	First Inversion
Key C:	C	F	G	C
Key G:	G	C	D	G
Key D:	D	G	A	D
Key A:	A	D	E	A
Key E:	E	A	B	E

Progression:	I	IImin	V	I
	First Inversion	**First Inversion**	**Root Position**	**First Inversion**
Key C:	C	Dmin	G	C
Key G:	G	Amin	D	G
Key D:	D	Emin	A	D
Key A:	A	Bmin	E	A
Key E:	E	F♯min	B	E

Progression:	I	VImin	IV	V	I
	First Inversion	**Second Inversion**	**Root Position**	**Second Inversion**	**First Inversion**
Key C:	C	Amin	F	G	C
Key G:	G	Emin	C	D	G
Key D:	D	Bmin	G	A	D
Key A:	A	F♯min	D	E	A
Key E:	E	C♯min	A	B	E

Progression:		I	VImin	IImin	V	I
		First Inversion	Second Inversion	First Inversion	Root Position	First Inversion
Key	C:	C	Amin	Dmin	G	C
	G:	G	Emin	Amin	D	G
	D:	D	Bmin	Emin	A	D
	A:	A	F♯min	Bmin	E	A
	E:	E	C♯min	F♯min	B	E

Progression:		I	IIImin	IV	I
		Root Position	Second Inversion	Second Inversion	Root Position
Key	C:	C	Emin	F	C
	G:	G	Bmin	C	G
	D:	D	F♯min	G	D
	A:	A	C♯min	D	A
	E:	E	G♯min	A	E

TRANSPOSING WITH MOVEABLE CHORD SHAPES

Practice the following chart in its original key, C major. Then, choose a different common key from the previous tables, and use the Roman numerals to find the moveable triad shapes that correspond to the transposition. Now, think about this: what if you need to play this song in a key we haven't studied, like B♭? You can do this, using moveable triad shapes. First, you'll write out the E♭ major scale and the Roman numerals for the diatonic triads. For reference, the major and minor triads in the key of B♭ major are: B♭ (I), Cmin (IImin), Dmin (IIImin), E♭ (IV), F (V), Gmin (VImin). Now, find the moveable triad shapes in E♭ major that correspond to the following chart, and play through them.

Wisdom

4/4 ‖: C G | Amin F | C G | F C :‖

I V VImin IV I V IV I

FIG. 10.3. "Wisdom" with Roman Numerals and Realizations

PRACTICE: ARRANGING WITH MOVEABLE TRIAD SHAPES

Now, create arrangements of the charts in part IV using moveable triad shapes, open chords, and power chords. If you are playing with a group, these three approaches to chord playing will expand the register of the rhythm section, creating low, middle, and high guitar parts. You can experiment further with texture by varying your strumming patterns and fingerpicking patterns in the different parts. To practice arranging with more charts, you can create your own, finding inspiration in the common chord progressions.

CHAPTER 11

Chords for Color and Motion

In this chapter, we'll explore chords that will take you beyond the basics of music theory. These chords provide interest, motion, and color to chord progressions. They are: seventh chords; secondary dominants; and "slash," "add," and "sus" chords. When we discuss seventh chords, we'll cover the useful—and sometimes feared—barre chord shape. Barres add an interesting texture to rhythm guitar playing, and they are a useful tool for playing chords in multiple keys.

CHORD THEORY: SEVENTH CHORDS

Seventh chords are four-note chords. Like triads, the seventh chords are built and named in relation to scale degrees. To build seventh chords with the major scale, add a fourth note on top of the chord, stacking one more note from the scale in an interval of a third. Like triads, seventh chords built on the major scale each have a quality based on its scale degree that is represented by a Roman numeral and a chord symbol. Chords built on major scale degrees 1 and 4 are called *major seventh chords,* written with the Roman numerals as IMaj7 and IVMaj7. The chords built on scale degrees 2, 3, and 6 are called *minor seventh chords,* written as IImin7, IIImin7, and VImin7. The chord built on scale degree 5 is called a *dominant seventh chord* and is written as V7. The seventh chord built on scale degree 7 may be called by two different names: *min7♭5* or *half-diminished 7.*

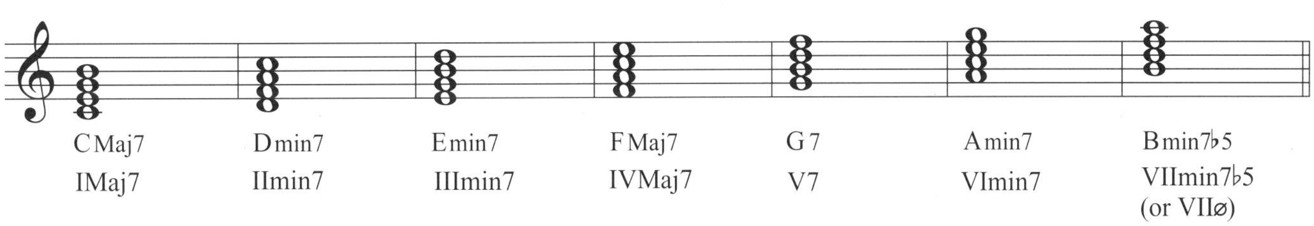

FIG. 11.1. Seventh Chords in C Major

In this chapter, we'll work with three types of seventh chords: the most common dominant and minor 7, and major 7 chords, often used in jazz, soul, and R&B styles. For expanded work with all seventh chords, refer to *Berklee Guitar Theory* (Berklee Press).

COMMON PROGRESSIONS WITH SEVENTH CHORDS

The following table shows common chord progressions that use seventh chords. Remember the common triad progressions from chapters 7 and 10? You'll notice that these progressions substitute seventh chords for some of the triads. Seventh chords add motion and color; dominant 7 chords add tension and intensify the motion of the progression. Minor 7 and major 7 chords add color and in some ways soften the movement of the progression.

Progression:	I	IV	V7	I
Key C:	C	F	G7	C
Key G:	G	C	D7	G
Key D:	D	G	A7	D
Key A:	A	D	E7	A
Key E:	E	A	B7	E

Progression:	I	IImin7	V7	I
Key C:	C	Dmin7	G7	C
Key G:	G	Amin7	D7	G
Key D:	D	Emin7	A7	D
Key A:	A	Bmin7	E7	A
Key E:	E	F♯min7	B7	E

Progression:	I	VImin7	IV	V7	I
Key C:	C	Amin7	F	G7	C
Key G:	G	Emin7	C	D7	G
Key D:	D	Bmin7	G	A7	D
Key A:	A	F♯min7	D	E7	A
Key E:	E	C♯min7	A	B7	E

Key	Progression:	IMaj7	IVMaj7	V7	IMaj7
Key	C:	CMaj7	FMaj7	G7	CMaj7
	G:	GMaj7	CMaj7	D7	GMaj7
	D:	DMaj7	GMaj7	A7	DMaj7
	A:	AMaj7	DMaj7	E7	AMaj7
	E:	EMaj7	AMaj7	B7	EMaj7

Key	Progression:	IMaj7	IIImin7	IVMaj7	IMaj7
Key	C:	CMaj7	Emin7	F7	CMaj7
	G:	GMaj7	Bmin7	C7	GMaj7
	D:	DMaj7	F♯min7	G7	DMaj7
	A:	AMaj7	C♯min7	D7	AMaj7
	E:	EMaj7	G♯min7	A7	EMaj7

Key	Progression:	IMaj7	VIMaj7	IImin7	V7	IMaj7
Key	C:	CMaj7	AMaj7	Dmin7	G7	CMaj7
	G:	GMaj7	EMaj7	Amin7	D7	GMaj7
	D:	DMaj7	BMaj7	Emin7	A7	DMaj7
	A:	AMaj7	F♯Maj7	Bmin7	E7	AMaj7
	E:	EMaj7	C♯Maj7	F#min7	B7	EMaj7

Key	Progression:	IMaj7	IImin7	V7	IMaj7
Key	C:	CMaj7	Dmin7	G7	CMaj7
	G:	GMaj7	Amin7	D7	GMaj7
	D:	DMaj7	Emin7	A7	DMaj7
	A:	AMaj7	Bmin7	E7	AMaj7
	E:	EMaj7	F♯min7	B7	EMaj7

OPEN CHORD VOICINGS FOR SEVENTH CHORDS

Many dominant and minor 7 chords can be played with open chord shapes. In the following set of chord diagrams, you'll see many we've covered, and a few new shapes. Learn these open chord shapes, and use them to practice the first three common seventh chord progressions.

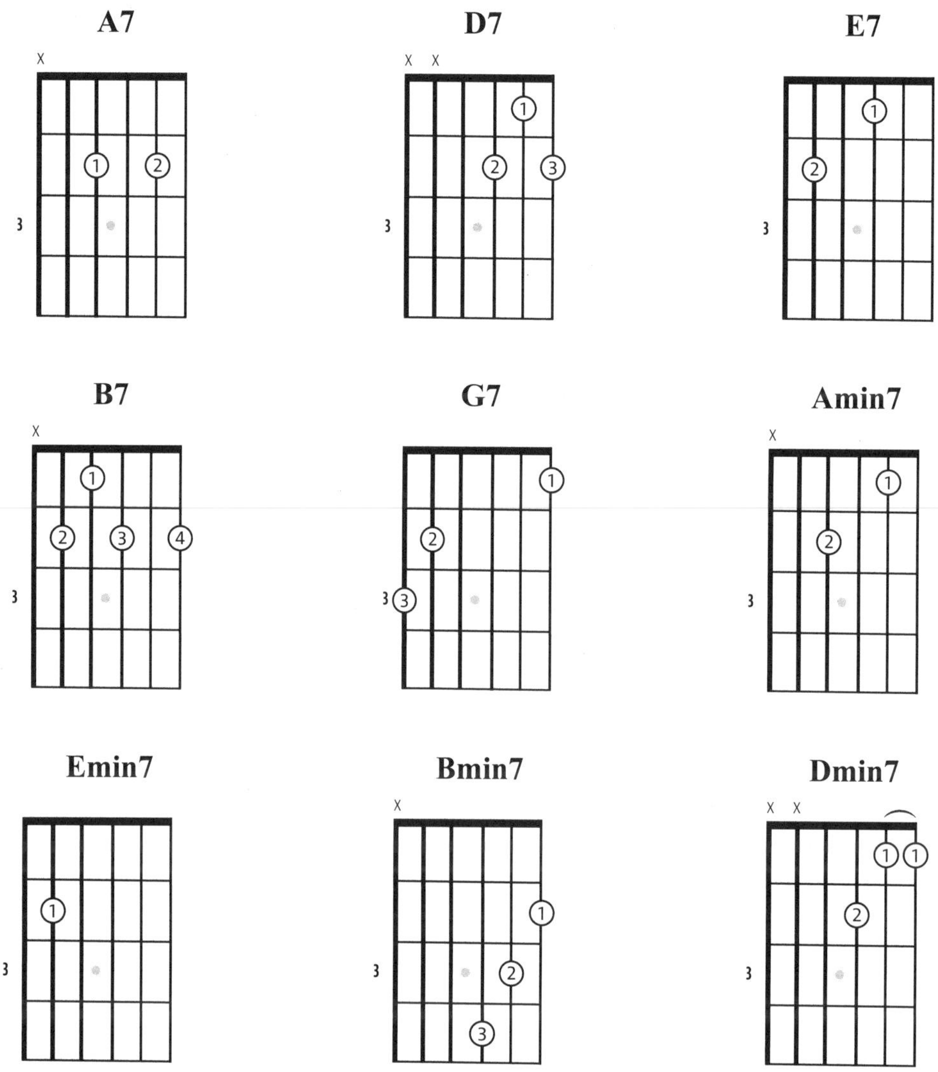

FIG. 11.2. Open Chord Diagrams: Dominant and Minor Seventh Chords

BARRE CHORDS: SHAPES WITH ROOTS ON STRING ⑥

Dominant, minor, and major 7 chords and triads can be fretted on the guitar as "barre" chord shapes. Major 7 chords, in particular, usually require a barre to be fretted, because of the chord construction.

A barre chord shape is made of a power chord on the bottom two strings and an open chord shape fretted above. Your first finger on your fretting hand *barres* across the fret that contains the bass note of the chord. Like your moveable triad shapes, barre chords are moveable shapes.

Barre chords that have their root note on string ⑥ are called *E shape* chords. This means that you'll play the bass note on string ⑥, barre that fret with your first finger, and then fret an E, Emin, E7, or Emin7 chord above it. The moveable Maj7 chord voicing is an exception in this set of chord shapes; you'll fret your bass note and an Amin chord shape, and you will not need to barre. Even though you are fretting E shapes, the name and sound of the chord corresponds to the bass note you're fretting. To create different chords, you'll move the barre chord shape to different roots. Take a look at the barre chord shapes with roots on string ⑥ in figure 10.3. Because our bass note here is G on the 3rd fret, these chords in figure 11.3 are G, Gmin, GMaj7, G7, Gmin7. The circled numbers in the chord diagrams indicate suggested fingerings.

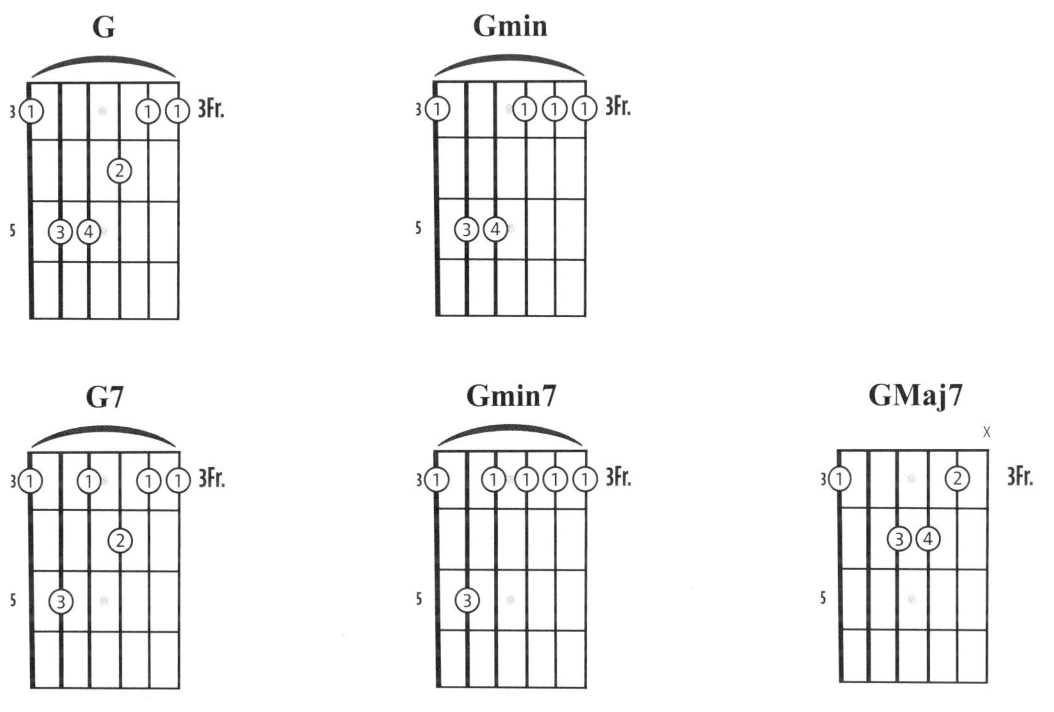

FIG. 11.3. Barre Chords on ⑥

BARRE CHORDS: SHAPES WITH ROOTS ON STRING ⑤

Barre chords that have their root note on string ⑤ are called *A shape* chords. This means that you'll play the bass note on string ⑤, barre that fret with your first finger, and then fret an A, Amin, A7, or Amin7 chord above it. Change one note from the A7 shape to fret AMaj7. Even though you are fretting A shapes, the name and sound of the chord corresponds to the bass note you're fretting.

Because our bass note here is C on the 3rd fret, these chords in figure 11.4 are C, Cmin, CMaj7, C7, Cmin7. To create different chords, you'll move the barre chord shape to different roots.

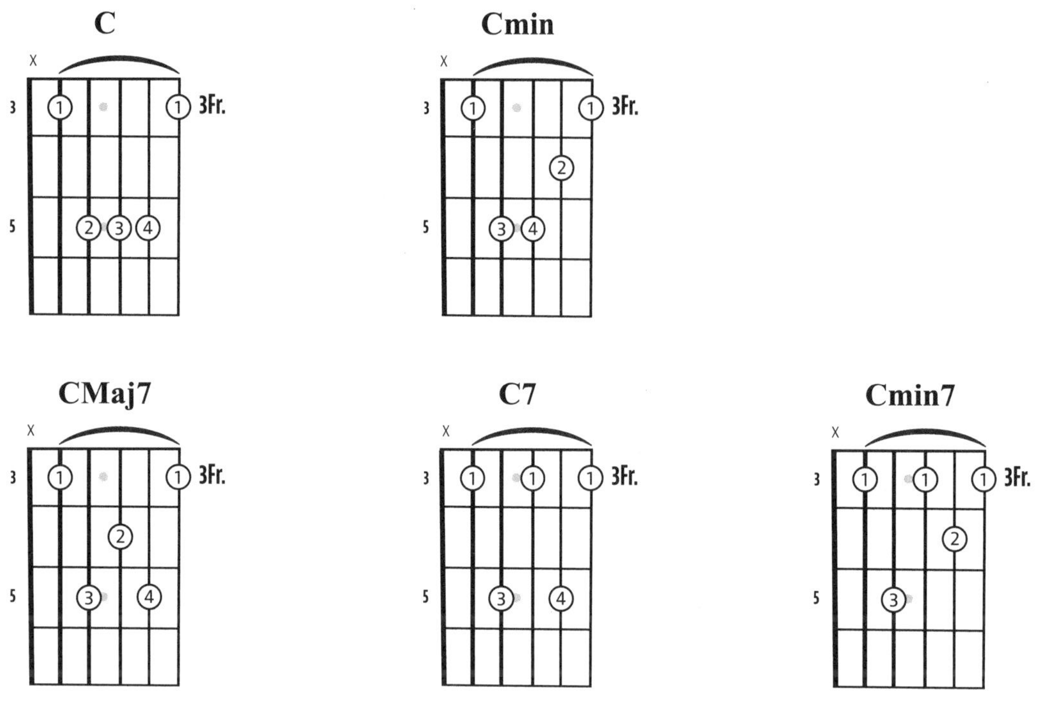

FIG. 11.4. Barre Chords on ⑤

PRACTICE BARRE CHORDS

Barre chords are physically challenging to practice. Move slowly, consider your position and technique, and build up your strength over time. Practice the barre chords rooted on ⑥ and ⑤ separately, and then practice shifting in a song chart.

To practice barre chords rooted on string ⑥:

1. Place the first finger of your fretting hand across the 5th fret, and place your thumb on the back of the neck for balance.
2. Roll your first finger to the bony part on the thumb side, and press down on the strings. Let most of the weight come from hanging your arm down from the guitar neck—not from pressing into the neck with your thumb!
3. Now, fret an E chord shape with fingers 2, 3, 4 above the barre, making an A chord. Readjust the pressure on your barre finger to focus on the strings that are not used the E shape: ⑥, ②, ①, and strum the chord.
4. Relax your shape, rest your hand, and repeat three times.

Go through these steps with the barre chord shapes for Amin, AMaj7, A7, and Amin7.

Next, practice barre chord technique with chords rooted on string ⑤. Follow the same steps you practiced with the ⑥-string barres. Barre the 5th fret, and fret an A chord shape with fingers 2, 3, 4 above the barre, making a D chord. Repeat the practice steps for the barre chords Dmin, D7, Dmin7.

By learning barre chord shapes with roots on both ⑥ and ⑤, you'll be able to shift through chord progressions easily—just as you did with power chords in chapter 2. Practice shifting barres and listening to the distinctive colors of seventh chords by learning the chart "Happening" in figure 11.5.

Happening

4/4 ||: EMaj7 | EMaj7 | C♯min7 | C♯min7 :||

||: F♯min7 | F♯min7 | B7 | B7 :||

FIG. 11.5. Chart with Major 7, Minor 7, Dominant 7, "Happening"

SECONDARY DOMINANTS

As you know from chapter 7, the chord built on the 5th degree of the major scale is called the "dominant." Functionally, the V chord leads the ear to the tonic chord (the I) of that key. Sometimes in a song, you'll hear an unexpected dominant chord, built on a different scale degree, and followed by a major or minor chord five scale degrees below. In these cases, the unexpected dominant is momentarily tonicizing the following chord, and is called a "secondary dominant." Secondary dominants create a momentary key change in a piece of music.

Because a secondary dominant tonicizes a chord other than the tonic of the home key, we identify it in Roman numerals as the dominant of its own tonic—for example, "the five of five," written as V7/V. The most common secondary dominants you'll see and hear are the V7/V and V7/VImin. Most often, a secondary dominant resolves to its tonic. Sometimes, a composer will choose not to progress in that way, creating an added surprise.

Practice: Secondary Dominants

Practice each of these charts, using open chords, triads, or barres, and listen to the secondary dominants.

Folk Song (V/V)

4/4 ||: D G | E7 | A :||

I IV | V/V | V

Prayer (V/VImin)

4/4 (repeat)

C	Amin	F	G	E	Amin
I	VImin	IV	V	V/VImin	VImin

Acceptance (V/V)

4/4 (repeat)

C	F	C	F
I	IV	I	IV
D	**F**	**C**	**F**
V/V	IV	I	IV

FIG. 11.6. Secondary Dominant Progressions

SLASH CHORDS

Slash chords are literally written with a slash mark in the chord symbol. They direct you to play the indicated chord with a bass note other than its tonic. When you use slash chords, you can incorporate bass lines in your rhythm guitar playing. Fret the open chord before the slash, and the bass note written after the slash. Take a look at these examples of these slash-chord diagrams, with suggested fingerings marked.

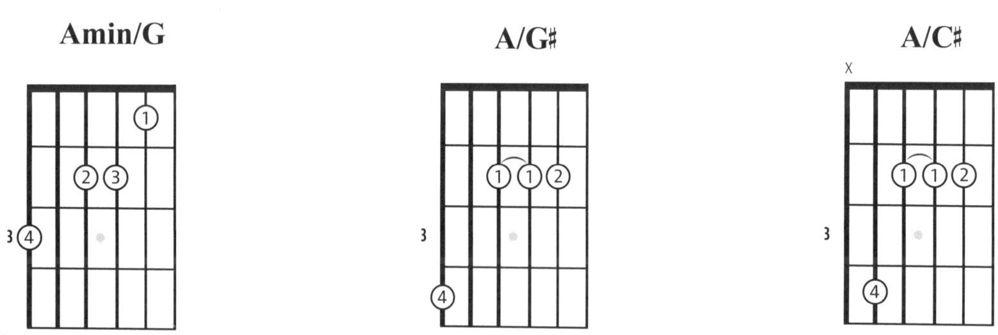

FIG. 11.7. Slash Chord Diagrams

PRACTICE: SLASH CHORDS

Practice slash chords in the context of a chord progression. The trickiest part of playing slash chords is the fingering. Find a fingering that will allow you to play both the bass note and the chord. One strategy is to play the bass note and then strum the chord. This will give you the opportunity to sound both, and shift your fretting hand position more easily.

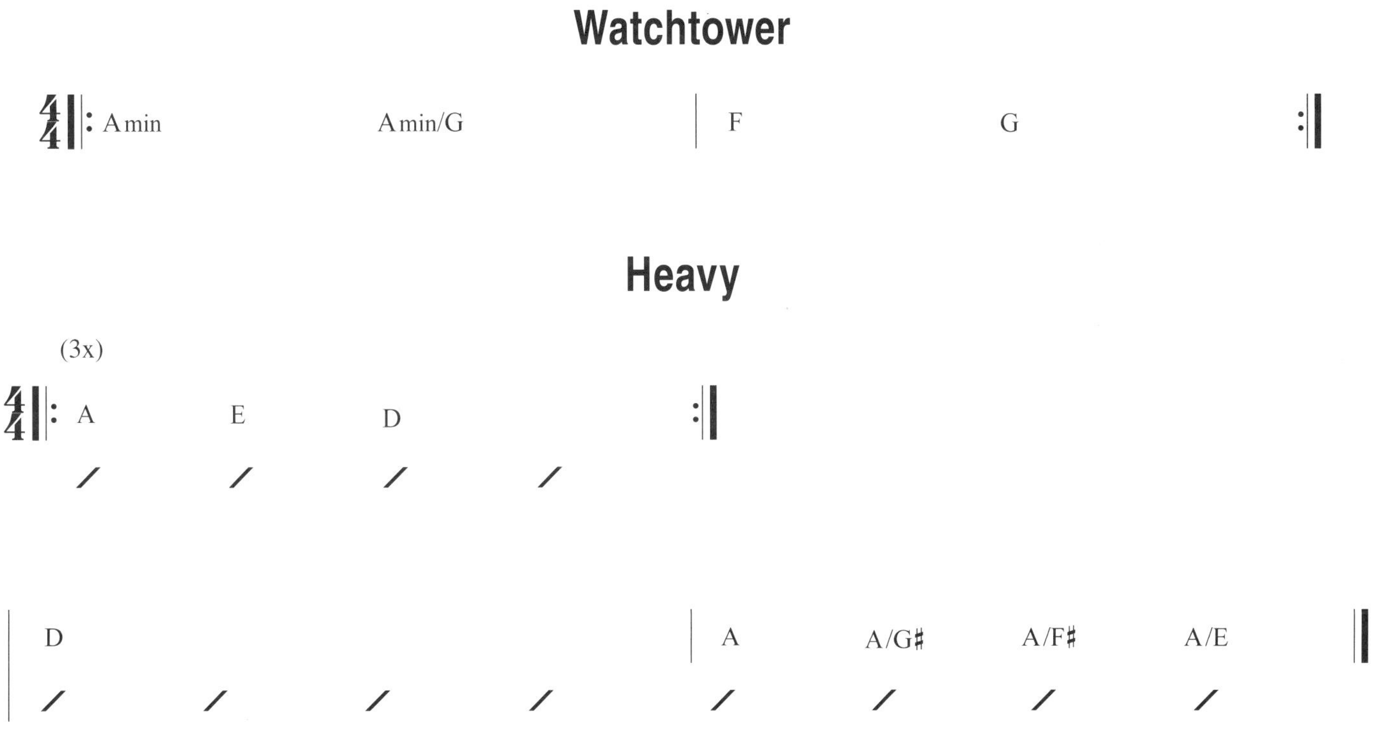

FIG. 11.8. Slash Chords, "Watchtower" and "Heavy"

"SUS" AND "ADD" CHORDS

Sus and *add* chords add interesting colors to your triads by adding another note from the scale or by substituting a scale tone for a triad note. In music theory, the difference between sus and add chords is their function: the sus chord contains a suspension note, which wants to move back to the note of the original triad. The add chord does not necessarily move back to the unaltered triad in the progression.

The most common sus chords are sus2 and sus4. In these chords, the third of the triad is replaced with the second or fourth notes of the scale from which the triad is built. This means that Dsus2 is built with the notes D, E, A. Dsus4 is built with the notes D, G, A. Look at the diagrams for these two chords compared to the open D chord, and listen to the difference as you play them.

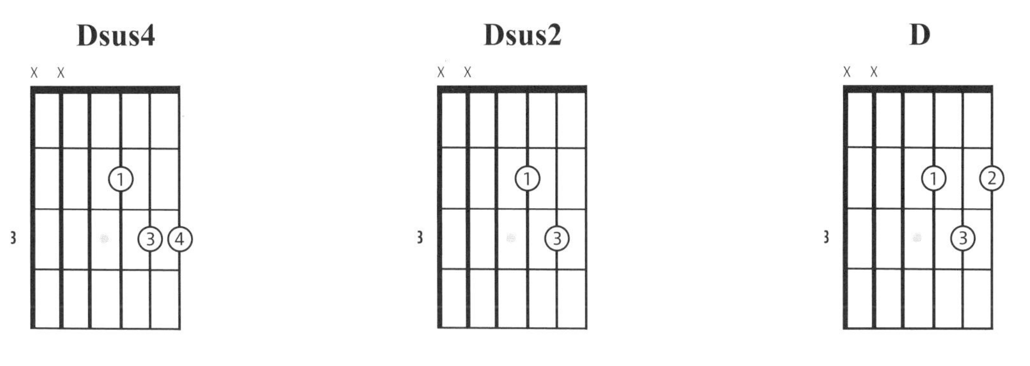

FIG. 11.9. Dsus Chords

A common add chord is add9. Add9 chords add in the second note of the scale to a triad, from which the chord is built an octave up—so that it is in the higher register of the chord voicing. Take a look at the chord diagram in figure 11.10, for Cadd9: C E G D. Listen to the sound of the add9 compared to the C major triad.

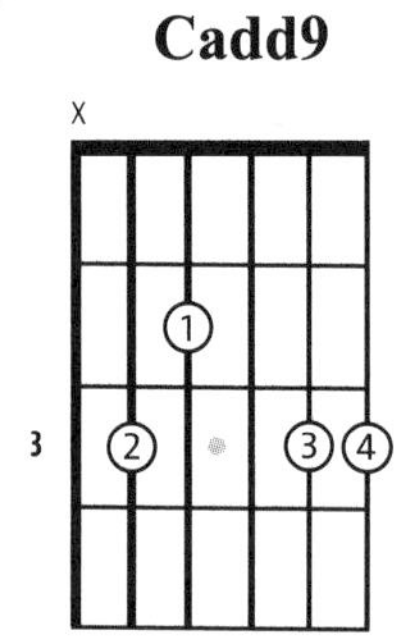

FIG. 11.10. Cadd9

PRACTICE: SUS AND ADD CHORDS

Practice this chord progression that incorporates the sus and add chords you've just learned. This progression uses a common quick change on the Dsus4 D Dsus2 D part of the progression that you will recognize if you've listened to a lot of strummers.

Closer

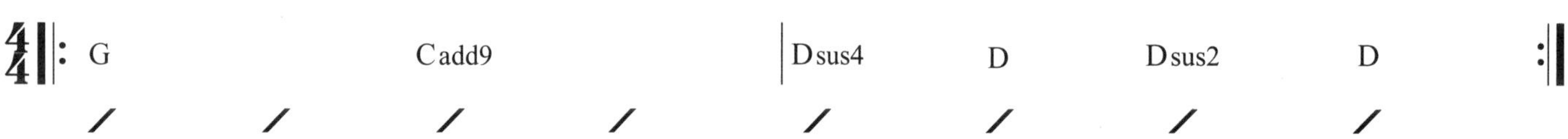

FIG. 11.11. Chart with Sus and Add Chords, "Closer"

PRACTICE: ARRANGING RHYTHM PARTS WITH BARRES

As you become comfortable playing barres, they become one more option—adding to the power chords, open chords, and moveable triad shapes in your chord-shape tool box. You also have the color and motion properties of the seventh, secondary dominant, slash, sus, and add chords to play with. Go to the charts in part IV, and experiment with arranging layered rhythm guitar parts. Now, if you are invited to play in a key like E♭ or B♭—one that does not use open chord shapes—you'll have power chords, triad shapes, and barre chords to use creatively! Try this in your own music as well.

CHAPTER 12

Basic Blues

Learning about the blues is a great way to play with others and learn about an essential style in American music. The blues has authenticities that define the style: signature forms, dominant-based harmony, pentatonic-based melodic structure, and distinctive rhythmic grooves. This chapter will focus on the most common twelve-bar blues forms played in the key of A, the "shuffle" rhythmic groove, and the "blues scale."

TWELVE-BAR MAJOR BLUES FORM

The most common blues form is the *twelve-bar blues*. This blues form can be played as a major or a minor, and in this chapter, we'll cover the major blues. The form consists of a twelve-bar chord progression, played in four with a backbeat emphasis, and organized in three four-bar phrases. In the major blues, the chords used are I, IV, V. Unlike songs in a major key, the major blues uses dominant voicings on all harmonies: I7, IV7, V7. The two most common twelve-bar blues forms are the "long" (or "long form") and the "quick change" forms.

The twelve-bar blues form in figure 12.1, is called the "long form," because the I chord is played for the entire first four-bar phrase.

I7	I7	I7	I7
IV7	IV7	I7	I7
V7	IV7	I7	V7

FIG. 12.1. Long Change Blues Form

The "quick change" twelve-bar blues form is different from the long form in one way: the IV chord is played in the second bar of the first four-bar phrase—a quick change from the I chord in the first phrase.

4/4			
I7	IV7	I7	I7
IV7	IV7	I7	I7
V7	IV7	I7	V7

FIG. 12.2. Quick Change Blues Form

Note that the last chord of the twelve-bar blues is a V chord. Ending the form on V is called a "turnaround," because it literally turns our ear's expectation around to the beginning of the form for the next verse. The last time through the form, you'll play a I chord to end.

RHYTHMIC FEEL: SHUFFLE AND STRAIGHT-SHUFFLE

Shuffle Feel

The "shuffle" groove (or feel) is associated with the blues. When you play a shuffle, you'll stretch the first eighth note of each beat and accent the second eighth-note, the off-beat. Acoustic blues players in particular play the folk strum in this feel, using open chords or barre chords. The "up" strum on the "and of 2" gets a heavy accent. Muting the strings on the downbeats will bring out the accents even more.

4/4			
A7	D7	A7	A7

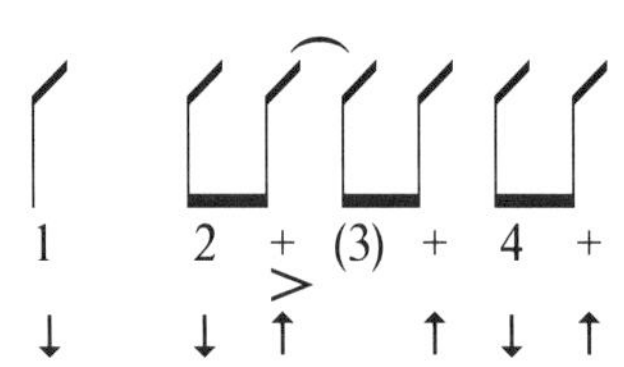

D7	D7	A7	A7
E7	D7	A7	E7

FIG. 12.3. Blues in a Shuffle Folk Strum

Shuffle Power Chord Pattern

In both electric and acoustic blues, the shuffle groove is often played with a power chord voicing and strumming pattern. You'll strum power chords in an eighth-note shuffle rhythm, adding one additional note on the backbeat. For a blues in A, there are two options for fretting this pattern, the open shuffle and the closed shuffle.

Open Shuffle

In the "open shuffle," you'll fret the power chords by using one open string on each chord (A, D, E) and fret the second note on the upper adjacent string with your first finger. You'll strum both strings together in eighth notes, and fret the "shuffle" note one whole step above on the upper adjacent string with your third finger, playing it on beats 2 and 4.

FIG. 12.4. Open Shuffle Chart for Each Chord in Blues in A

Closed Shuffle

In the "closed shuffle," you'll fret the power chord traditionally. Fret the I chord (A) with the root on ⑥, and the IV and V chords (D and E) with their roots on ⑤. Strum both strings together in eighth notes, and fret the note one whole step above on the upper adjacent string with your fourth finger—playing it on beats 2 and 4.

FIG. 12.5. Closed Shuffle for Each Chord in Blues in A

Straight Eighths Shuffle

You'll often hear the straight-eighths approach to the shuffle pattern in rock tunes that are influenced by the blues. To create the straight-eighth feel, play the shuffle pattern in an eighth-note strumming pattern that divides the beat equally in half—not stretched, as in the shuffle feel. Accent the backbeat as you play. Notice that the rhythmic notation looks identical to the typical shuffle. You will create the difference in feel by the way you play the eighth-note rhythm.

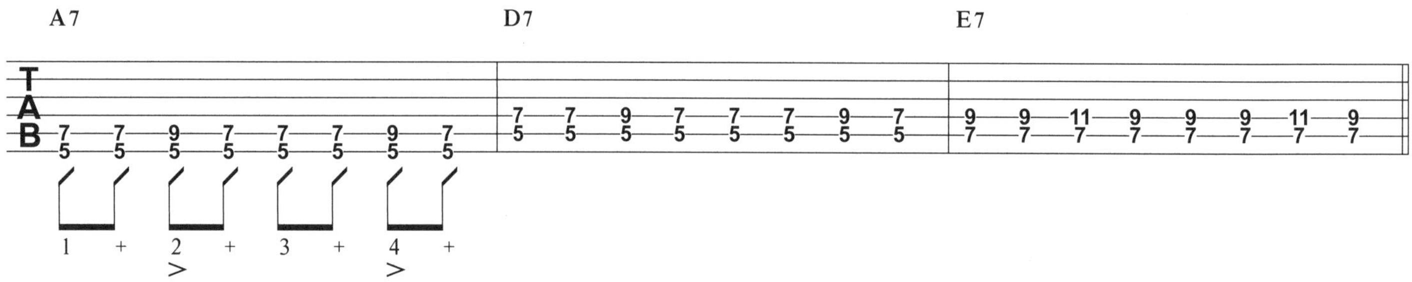

FIG 12.6. Straight Eighths Shuffle for Each Chord in Blues in A

THE BLUES SCALE

The blues scale adds one note to the minor pentatonic scale. The minor pentatonic scale, you'll remember, is scale degrees 1 ♭3 4 5 ♭7 (compared to the major scale). The blues scale adds one note to this scale, the ♭5, making it: 1 ♭3 4 ♭5 5 7. To practice this, revisit the minor pentatonic patterns you learned in chapter 5, and add the ♭5 note. Figure 12.7 shows the five patterns of the A minor pentatonic with the ♭5 added.

Blues Pattern	A Blues
5	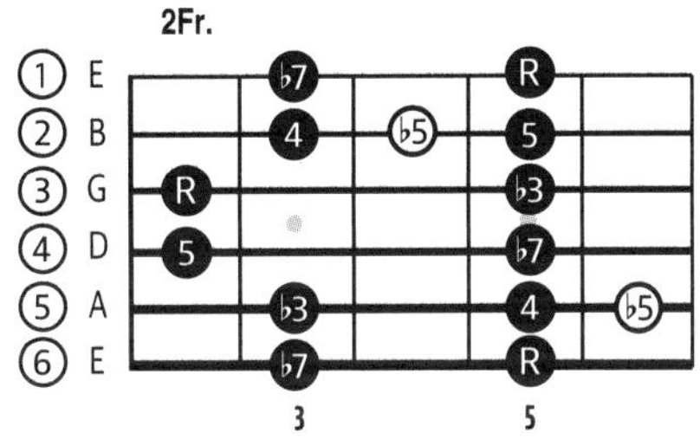
1	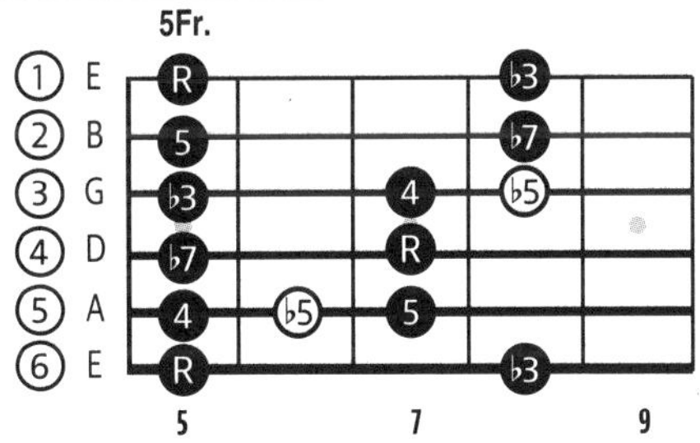
2	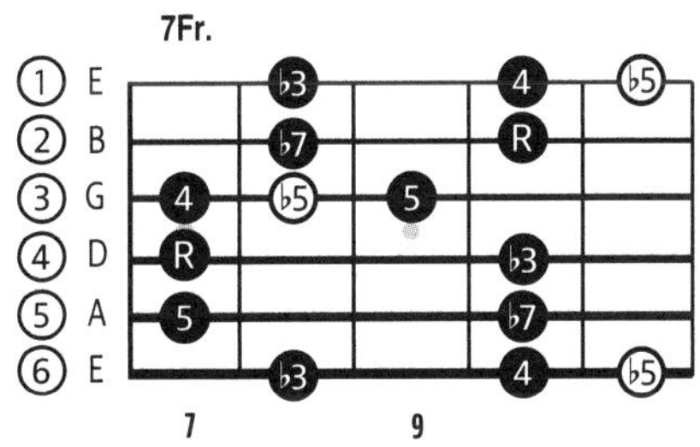
3	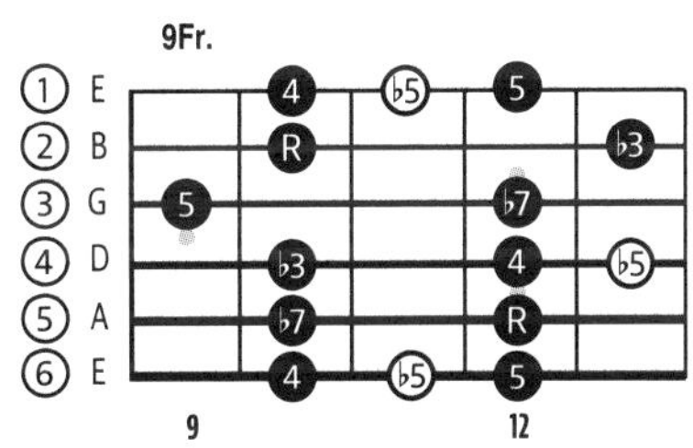
4	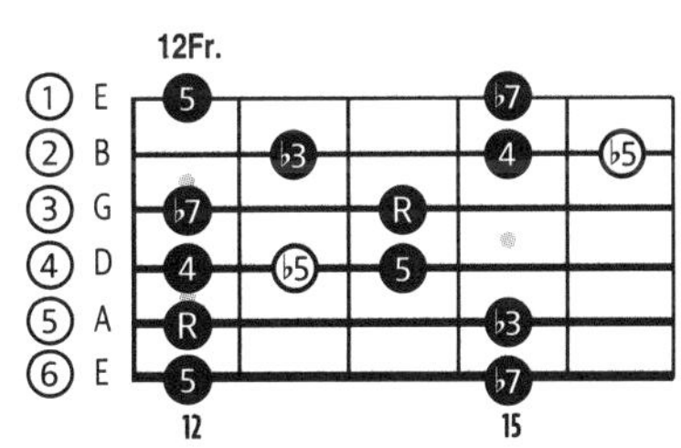

FIG. 12.7. A Blues Scale Patterns

PRACTICE: SOLOING ON A TWELVE-BAR BLUES IN A

To solo on the twelve-bar blues in A, you can use the blues scale and the minor pentatonic patterns. Because the twelve-bar form is divided into three four bar phrases, you will improvise three melodic ideas—one with each four-bar phrase. One common approach to phrasing in the blues is to play one melody with the first four-bar phrase, repeat it in the second, and answer it with the third. This type of phrasing form is called AAB. The melodies can be simple. It is the way that you play the melodies, using the parameters of sound, that make them effective.

Record a twelve-bar blues in A, playing the form at least four times. Choose your approach: Open chords? The shuffle pattern? Straight? Using the first pattern of the A blues scale, improvise melodies with your rhythm part. Follow the AAB phrasing pattern by playing an idea with the first four bars, repeating it with the second, and answering it with a different idea with the third.

PRACTICE: PLAYING AN A BLUES

Now that you are practicing the basics, you're ready to pull the materials together, play with others, and deepen your listening. First, become familiar with each of the approaches in this chapter. Next, seek out a few musicians to play with you. To invite others to play in the blues form you expect, you'll ask in a specific way. The twelve-bar form is so common, they'll likely assume that length of form. You can ask for the quick change, the groove, tempo, and the key: "Let's play blues in A, with the quick change, and a medium shuffle." Others may reference the style of a specific recording: "Let's do a blues in A, long form, slow-shuffle, in the style of Jimi Hendrix's 'Red House.'" If you're asked to play that, now you'll know what to do!

For more work with the blues, take yourself on a listening adventure, and check out Mike Williams's books *Berklee Blues Guitar Technique* (Berklee Press, 2014) and the *Berklee Blues Guitar Songbook* (Berklee Press, 2010).

Part IV

Practice Charts

Now that you've built your guitar foundation, you have a wealth of materials and techniques to work on in your practice routine. Each day when you practice, rotate technical warm-ups, chord voicings, and scale patterns—always working on your tone and breathing. Spend time reviewing the music theory as applied to these materials: sing your melodies as you improvise, notate your improvisations, work on your rhythms, develop your reading, and analyze and transpose the chord progressions from the songs you play. Next, apply this work to specific song charts. The examples in each chapter will focus your attention on specifics, and the charts in this section will allow you to make creative choices drawing from lessons in multiple parts of the book.

Practice this group of charts, using each chart's preliminary information as a guide. Materials not specified are your creative choice, including strumming patterns, fingerpicking patterns, groove/feel, tempo, and phrasing.

For each chart, create and record a rhythm guitar part, with one track or multiple layered tracks. Next, play a lead guitar part with improvisation, incorporating written riffs and melodies when those are included. Create as many different versions of each chart as you can by varying your choices. How much contrast can you create? What materials and techniques bring out your musical voice as you play?

As you play these charts and create your own arrangements, you may hear the echoes of hit songs that use similar chord progressions. Many popular songs are similar in this way. Their unique qualities lie in the musician's creative choices. What choices will you make as a player to honor tradition? To create something new with a familiar "sound?"

Enjoy your short-term and long-term journey with these materials, and whichever path with the guitar comes next for you!

Heaven

Key: G major **Solo:** G major pentatonic
Chord Voicings: power, open, triad, barre

4/4 ||: G D | Amin |

| G D | C :||

Watchtower

Key: A minor **Solo:** A minor pentatonic
Chord Voicings: power, open, triad, barre

4/4 ||: Amin G | F G :||
/ / / / | / / / /

Wisdom

Key: C major **Solo:** C major pentatonic
Chord Voicings: power, open, triad, barre

Verse

4/4 ||: C G | Amin F |

| C G | F C :||

Chorus

4/4 ||: Amin G | F C :||

Acceptance

Key: C major

Chord Voicings: power, open, triad, barre

Solo: C major pentatonic

Verse

Chorus

| C | F | C | F |

| C | F | D | F |

| C | F | C | F ||

Happening

Key: E major

Chord Voicings: power, open, triad, barre

Solo: E major pentatonic/E major

Rhythm: backbeat groove

4/4 ||: EMaj7 | EMaj7 | C♯min7 | C♯min7 :||

||: F♯min7 | F♯min7 | B7 | B7 :||

Heavy

Key: A major

Chord Voicings: power, open, triad, barre

Solo: A major pentatonic

Intro

4/4 A | A ||

Verse

(4x)

4/4 |: Amin C♯min | D A :|

Chorus

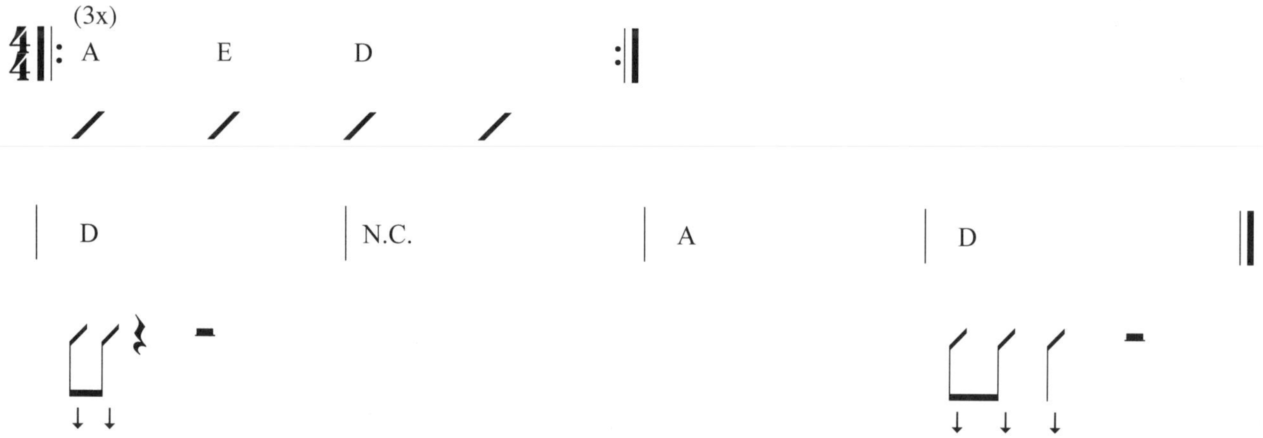

Happy Birthday

Key: C major

Chord Voicings: power, open, triad, barre

Solo: C major pentatonic or C major pentatonic

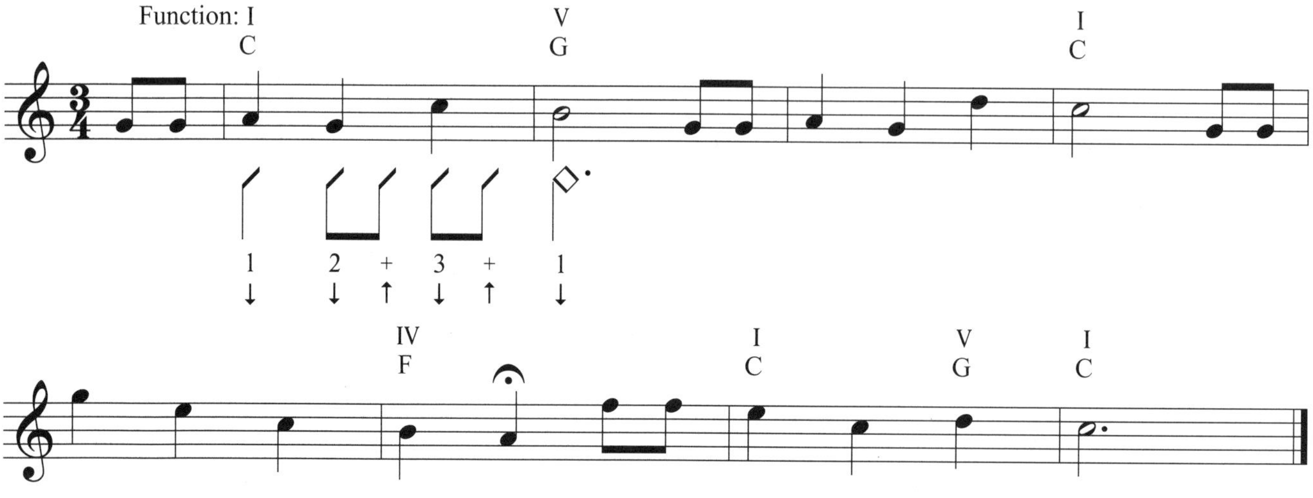

This transposable chart features scale degrees under rhythm notation. A line above a degree indicates that it is played lower than the root. Learn this song in several keys!

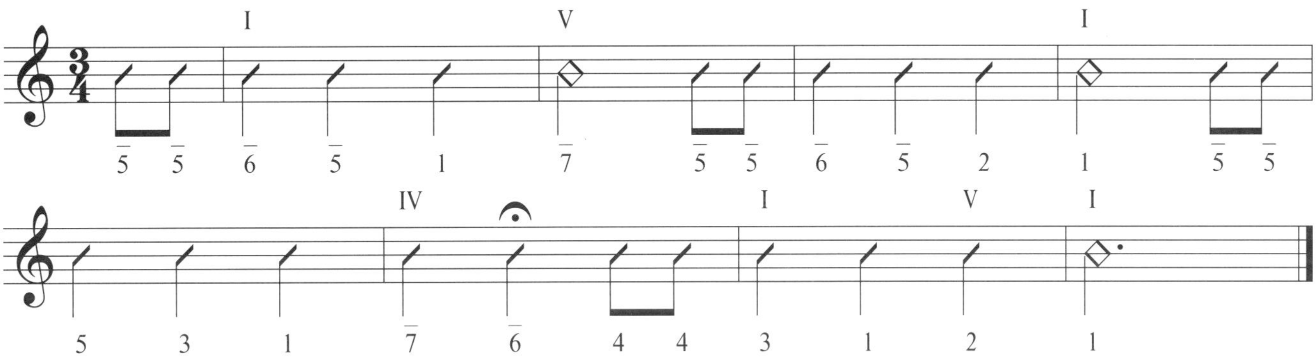

Progression:	I	V	I	IV	I	V	I
Key C:	C	G	C	F	C	G	C
Key G:	G	D	G	C	G	D	G
Key D:	D	A	D	G	D	A	D
Key A:	A	E	A	D	A	E	A
Key E:	E	B	E	A	E	B	E

People

Key: D major
Chord Voicings: power, open, triad, barre
Solo: D major pentatonic
Rhythm: accents on beats 1 and the "and" of 2

Together

Key: Verse is D blues, chorus is D major

Chord Voicings: power

Solo: (Verse) D blues

Rhythm: Verse is straight eighths, backbeat groove; chorus has strongbeat feel

Riff:

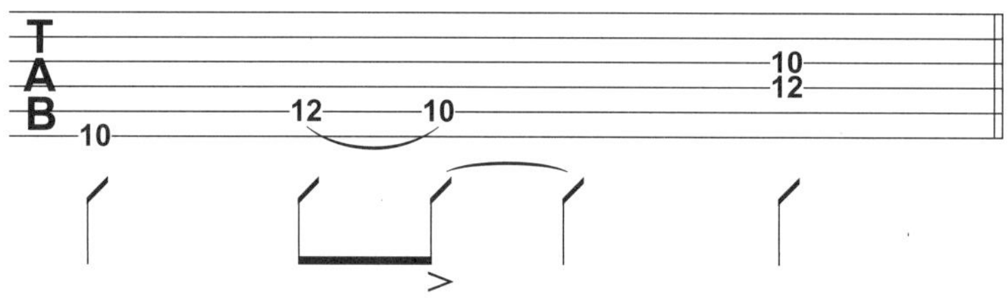

Verse

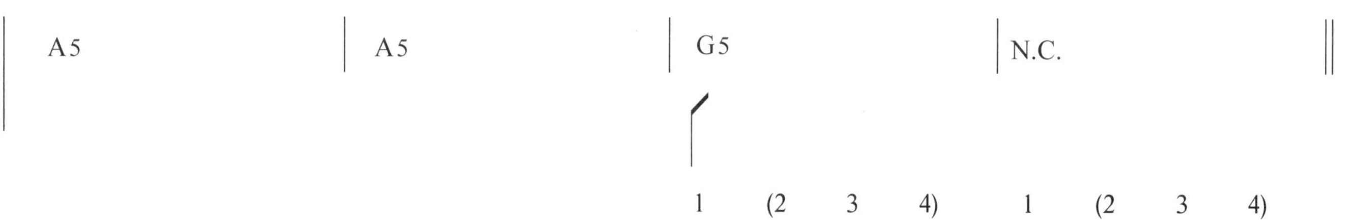

Chorus

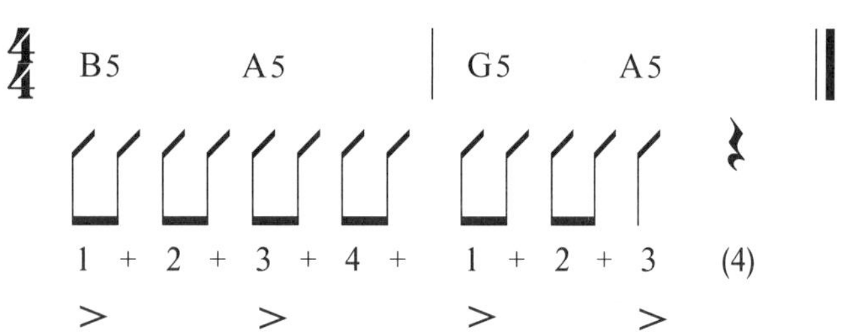

Prayer

Key: C major/A minor
Chord Voicings: power, open, triad, barre
Solo: C major pentatonic/A minor pentatonic
Fingerpicking pattern: notated for each open chord

CONCLUDING THOUGHT

Congratulations! As you have worked through this book, you have built a strong foundation for your guitar playing. You'll build on this foundation for years to come, learning from teachers, recordings, performances, and by playing with your friends. Whether you came to this material as an absolute beginner, or a player with some foundational gaps, I encourage you to revisit this material each day in your practice. Spend time, so that the data, concepts, and techniques become instinctual in your playing. Use this foundation as a place to build and explore from: in whatever style and creative approach you choose.

In the Berklee global guitar community, one of the most exciting things is to listen to the way in which each guitar player develops their artistry in every style and approach imaginable. Now, it's your turn to join in!

Good luck on your next steps!

ABOUT THE AUTHOR

Kim Perlak serves as the chair of the Guitar Department at Berklee College of Music. She is also the author of *Classical Technique for the Modern Guitarist* (Berklee Press), the curator of *Berklee Guitar Theory* (Berklee Press), and the co-curator of *Berklee Essential Guitar Songbook* (Berklee Press). Kim is the author and instructor for the online course *Beginning Guitar* for Berklee Online. Her approach to the guitar includes new music, education, and public service. Her performances of classical works, original pieces, and collaborations with jazz and traditional players have been featured on National Public Radio, at the Peabody Institute Fretfest, and on five recordings. Her projects combining performance, American music history, and educational outreach have been funded through grants from the Center for African American Southern Music and Yale Alumni Ventures.

Kim's collaborative guitar work with American veterans in the concert project "Ben & I Play for Peace" was honored by the PBS program *From the Top* as part of their Arts Leadership series, and was recognized by the U.S. House of Representatives. Today, the work of "Ben & I" continues in the Veterans Guitar Project, based in Austin, TX.

Kim serves on the boards of the Guitar Foundation of America, the Boston Classical Guitar Society, the D'Addario Education Advisory Board, and The Music and Health Institute at Berklee College of Music. Kim's current artistic work includes improvisation, composition, and course development as a soloist and in a duo with slide guitarist/Berklee guitar professor David Tronzo.

Kim holds degrees from The University of Texas at Austin (DMA '08), Yale University School of Music (MM '01), and Stetson University (BM '98), and a certificate of completion from the Harvard University Management Development Program (2014).

Kim concertizes on guitars by Thomas Humphrey and Kirk Sand, and uses D'Addario Strings.

ABOUT THE BERKLEE GUITAR DEPARTMENT

Berklee College of Music was the first institution of higher education to grant a degree with guitar as the principal instrument, in 1962. To this day, Berklee's Guitar Department remains the largest and most stylistically diverse guitar program in the world. We provide private instruction, labs, and ensembles in all styles, including: jazz, blues, rock, metal, funk, fingerstyle, classical, world music, modern improvisation, microtonal music, and the avant-garde.

Many of the world's most ground-breaking guitarists studied at Berklee, including Mike Stern, Leni Stern, Kevin Eubanks, John Mayer, Bill Frisell, Gillian Welch, Emily Remler, John Scofield, Steve Vai, St. Vincent, and Adrianne Lenker and Buck Meek of Big Thief. Our alumni community includes current and former faculty such as Mick Goodrick, Pat Metheny, Sheryl Bailey, Wayne Krantz, Tomo Fujita, David Tronzo, and Tim Miller.

To get involved with guitar at Berklee, through formal education in the department at the College or with studies at Summer Programs, through Global Initiatives, or Berklee Online, please visit: college.berklee.edu/guitar.

More Guitar Publications

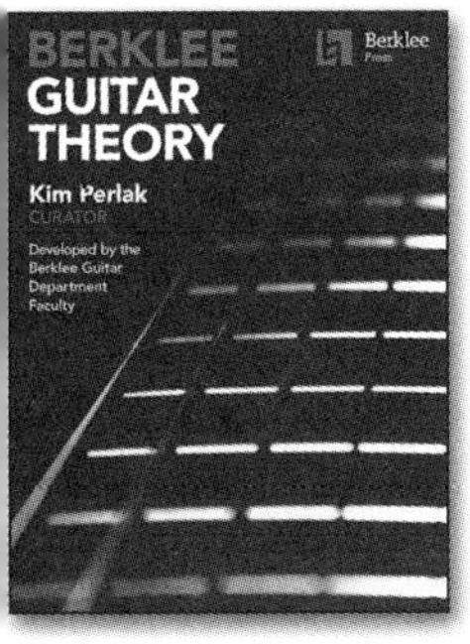

ADVANCED READING STUDIES FOR GUITAR
William Leavitt
50449500 Book $24.99

BEBOP GUITAR SOLOS
Michael Kaplan
00121703 Book $22.99

BERKLEE BASIC GUITAR
William Leavitt
50449460 Phase 1 Book $14.99
50449470 Phase 2 Book $17.99

BERKLEE BASIC UKULELE
Karen Hogg
00581260 Book/Online Audio $16.99

BERKLEE BLUES GUITAR SONGBOOK
Michael Williams
50449593 Book/Online Audio $29.99

BERKLEE ESSENTIAL GUITAR SONGBOOK
Kim Perlak, Sheryl Bailey, and Members of the Berklee Guitar Department Faculty
00350814 Book $22.99

BERKLEE GUITAR CHORD DICTIONARY
Rick Peckham
50449546 Book - Jazz $16.99
50449596 Book - Rock $12.99

BERKLEE GUITAR CHORDS 101
Rick Peckham
00300636 Book/Online Audio $29.99

BERKLEE GUITAR STYLE STUDIES
Jim Kelly
00200377 Book/Online Media $24.99

BERKLEE GUITAR THEORY
Kim Perlak and Members of the Berklee Guitar Department Faculty
00276326 Book $26.99

BERKLEE JAZZ STANDARDS FOR SOLO GUITAR
John Stein
50449653 Book/Online Audio $24.99

BERKLEE PRACTICE METHOD FOR GUITAR
Larry Baione
50449426 Book/CD $29.99

BERKLEE SOLO UKULELE
Karen Hogg
00327666 Book/Online Audio $16.99

BLUES GUITAR TECHNIQUE
Michael Williams
50449623 Book/Online Audio $29.99

THE CHORD FACTORY
Jon Damian
50449541 Book $29.99

CLASSICAL STUDIES FOR PICK-STYLE GUITAR
William Leavitt
50449440 Book $14.99

CLASSICAL TECHNIQUE FOR THE MODERN GUITARIST
Kim Perlak
00148781 Book/Online Audio $19.99

CONTEMPORARY JAZZ GUITAR SOLOS
Michael Kaplan
00143596 Book $16.99

COUNTRY GUITAR STYLES
Mike Ihde
00254157 Book/Online Audio $24.99

CREATIVE CHORDAL HARMONY FOR GUITAR
Mick Goodrick and Tim Miller
50449613 Book/Online Audio $24.99

FUNK/R&B GUITAR
Thaddeus Hogarth
50449569 Book/Online Audio $25.99

GUITAR SWEEP PICKING & ARPEGGIOS
Joe Stump
00151223 Book/Online Audio $24.99

THE GUITARIST'S GUIDE TO COMPOSING AND IMPROVISING
Jon Damian
50449497 Book/Online Audio $29.99

INTRODUCTION TO JAZZ GUITAR
Jane Miller
00125041 Book/Online Audio $26.99

JAZZ GUITAR FRETBOARD NAVIGATION
Mark White
00154107 Book/Online Audio $24.99

JAZZ GUITAR IMPROVISATION STRATEGIES
Steven Kirby
00274977 Book/Online Media $27.99

JAZZ IMPROVISATION FOR GUITAR
Garrison Fewell
50449594 Book/Online Audio - Harmonic Approach .. $29.99
50449503 Book/Online Audio - Melodic Approach $29.99

JAZZ SWING GUITAR
Jon Wheatley
00139935 Book/Online Audio $29.99

MELODIC RHYTHMS FOR GUITAR
William Leavitt
50449450 Book $17.99

Joe Stump's
METAL GUITAR CHOP SHOP
50449601 Book/Online Audio $19.99

MODAL VOICING TECHNIQUES FOR GUITAR
Rick Peckham
00151227 Book/Online Video $26.99

A MODERN METHOD FOR GUITAR
William Leavitt
50449400 Volume 1 Book $16.99
50449404 Volume 1 Book/Online Audio $27.99
00137387 Volume 1 Book/Online Video $27.99
50449410 Volume 2 Book $19.99
50448021 Volume 2 Book/Online Audio $26.99
50449420 Volume 3 Book $24.99
00292989 Volume 3 Book/Online Audio $24.99
50449468 Volumes 1-3 Book $44.99
00292990 Volumes 1-3 Book/Online Media $54.99

A MODERN METHOD FOR GUITAR SCALES
Larry Baione
00199318 Book $17.99

A MODERN METHOD FOR GUITAR SONGBOOKS
50449539 Jazz with Online Audio $22.99
50449624 Rock with CD $17.99

THE PRACTICAL JAZZ GUITARIST
Mark White
50449618 Book/Online Audio $29.99

THE PRIVATE GUITAR STUDIO HANDBOOK
Mike McAdam
00121641 Book $14.99

READING STUDIES FOR GUITAR
William Leavitt
50449490 Book $19.99

TRIADS FOR THE IMPROVISING GUITARIST
Jane Miller
00284857 Book/Online Audio $22.99

Visit your local music dealer or bookstore,
or go to **www.berkleepress.com**
Prices and availability subject to change without notice

HAL•LEONARD®
A Muse Group Company

Berklee Press

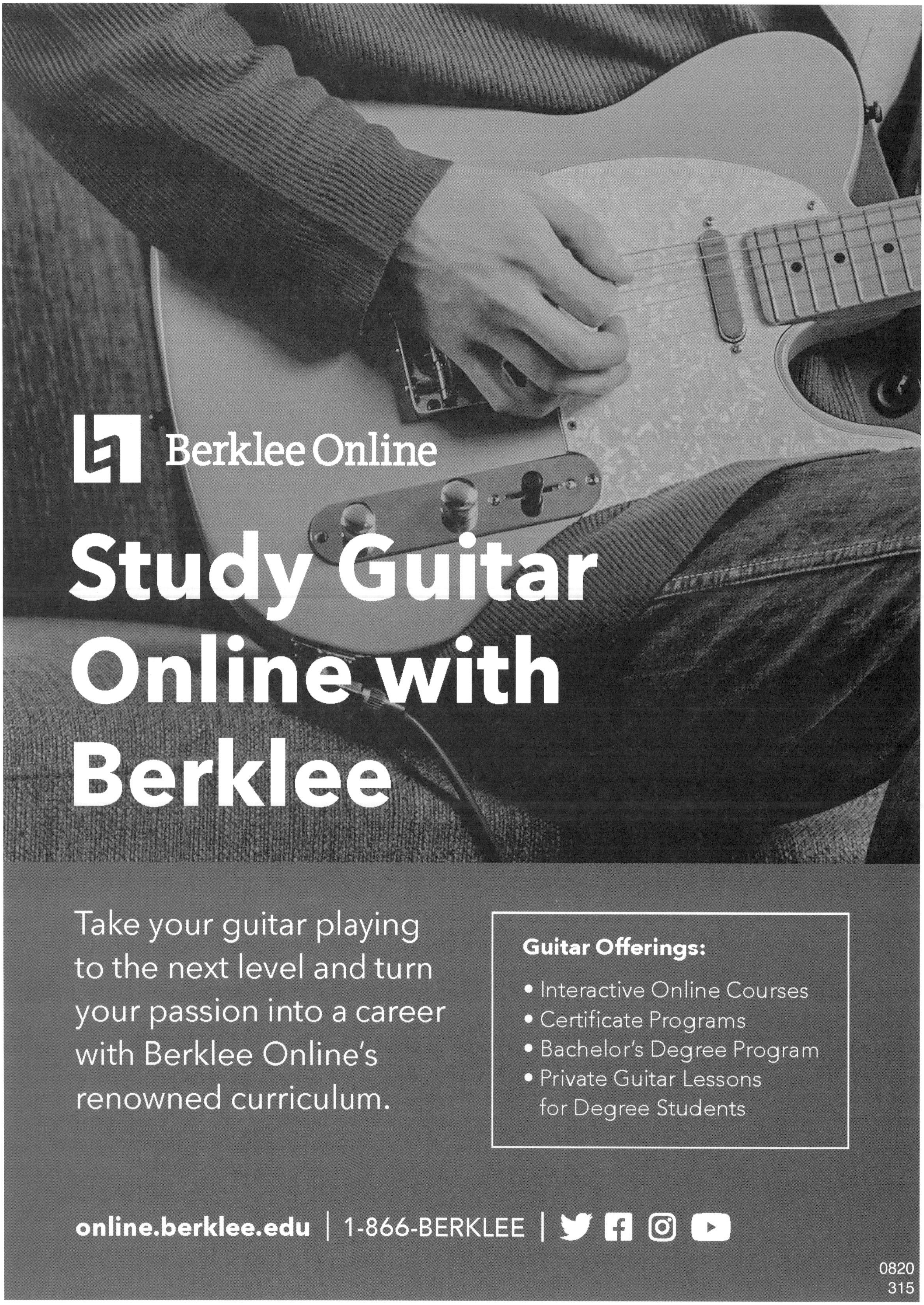
Berklee Online
Study Guitar Online with Berklee
Take your guitar playing to the next level and turn your passion into a career with Berklee Online's renowned curriculum.
Guitar Offerings:
• Interactive Online Courses
• Certificate Programs
• Bachelor's Degree Program
• Private Guitar Lessons for Degree Students
online.berklee.edu | 1-866-BERKLEE
0820
315